MW01073878

From At-Risk to At-Promise

From At-Risk to At-Promise

Academic Libraries Supporting Student Success

Amy E. Vecchione and Cathlene E. McGraw

LIBRARIES
UNLIMITED®

An Imprint of ABC-CLIO, LLC

Santa Barbara, California • Denver, Colorado

Copyright © 2023 by Amy E. Vecchione and Cathlene E. McGraw

All rights reserved. No part of this publication may be reproduced, stored in a retrieval system, or transmitted, in any form or by any means, electronic, mechanical, photocopying, recording, or otherwise, except for the inclusion of brief quotations in a review, without prior permission in writing from the publisher.

Library of Congress Cataloging-in-Publication Data

Names: Vecchione, Amy E., author. | McGraw, Cathlene E., author.
Title: From at-risk to at-promise : academic libraries supporting student
　　success / Amy E. Vecchione and Cathlene E. McGraw.
Description: Santa Barbara, California : Libraries Unlimited, [2023] |
　　Includes bibliographical references and index.
Identifiers: LCCN 2022027102 | ISBN 9781440876356 (paperback) |
　　ISBN 9781440876363 (ebook)
Subjects: LCSH: Academic libraries—United States. | Libraries and
　　students—United States. | BISAC: LANGUAGE ARTS & DISCIPLINES / Library
　　& Information Science / General | EDUCATION / Schools / Levels / Higher
Classification: LCC Z675.U5 V43 2023 | DDC 027.70973—dc23/eng/20220825
LC record available at https://lccn.loc.gov/2022027102

ISBN: 978-1-4408-7635-6 (print)
　　　 978-1-4408-7636-3 (ebook)

27　26　25　24　23　　　1　2　3　4　5

This book is also available as an eBook.

Libraries Unlimited
An Imprint of ABC-CLIO, LLC

ABC-CLIO, LLC
147 Castilian Drive
Santa Barbara, California 93117
www.abc-clio.com

This book is printed on acid-free paper ∞

Manufactured in the United States of America

Contents

Part Four   Conclusion

Introduction

Student populations in higher education are evolving as universities and colleges admit more varied demographics of students. As student populations in higher education are changing, many students require different services, programs, opportunities, and support in order to succeed. Many of the existing structures in higher education were designed and built for students from white middle- and upper-class economic status and from European cultures. As the demographics at universities change, librarians, staff, and faculty must work to evolve the existing services and structures to serve these new student populations.

Services and structures in libraries ought to evolve through a process of collaboration and assessment. Because the student demographics are shifting and, as a result, are presenting college campuses with new opportunities to serve students, this is a necessity. Meanwhile, higher education is also experiencing increased pressure to reduce budgets while serving more students. Some areas may be growing, while others are contracting. Within certain areas of the university, including libraries, academic advising, and other student services, budgets are becoming limited. It is challenging to evolve services without additional financial resources.

An additional pressure comes from all students' general point of view. Certainly, it can easily be assumed that most undergraduate students enroll in colleges and universities in order to graduate, though not all undergraduates succeed in this endeavor. Those undergraduate students who do graduate have new expectations for their college experience, as the world continues to change. One expectation is that of acquiring gainful employment immediately after graduation, a primary measure of success for some.

While structures do get put in place to best serve the students being admitted to college, students continue to have many needs. Some of these structures can, and should, grow in an organic fashion based on overlapping services from specific college units, shared understandings, and the needs of students. Throughout this book the reader will learn about how librarians and student success administrators can partner effectively to start this process.

Academic librarians and student success administrators can collaborate; together they can create additional pathways and opportunities for students who struggle to succeed. This book intends to provide a road map for library employees and student success administrators to initiate and develop discussions on college campuses to define and then address student needs. Student needs are emergent, and while all students need more services and support, new services may need to be tailored based on regional needs. Through a selection of case studies and historical context, readers will learn both how to define what student success looks like in their units and how to design custom services to address student barriers to that success.

Academic library employees include frontline staff, librarians, managers, and administrators. On-campus student success administrators are professionals who include advisors, student counselors, as well as managers. These two main audiences, library employees and student success professionals, share a common cause of serving students, including those who are at the margins of college campus demographics. Readers will acquire skills to enhance student success initiatives and strengthen collaborations with one another. A tertiary group of potential collaborators includes higher education employees from student success programs such as academic affairs, admissions, and student retention—anyone who collaborates with internal or external stakeholders. An internal stakeholder could be someone from one's own team, and external stakeholders could be someone from a different division or college from your team. External stakeholders may also include individuals from outside the college or university.

This book draws from lived experiences from the perspectives of librarians and student success administrators who have for decades collaboratively designed new services to help strengthen student services. Certain parts of the book will help provide new definitions of student success customized to the individuals or groups mentioned.

In Chapter 1, we present the lens by which we view this problem. By presenting the core issue, it can be more effective to help improve outcomes for students. Through this understanding, it can be more effective to make changes within higher education that situate the student experience to enhance their success. Then, part 1 of this book lays out the history of student success, focusing on those who have been let into the university and the barriers they faced over time. Student populations on campus are expanding to include more diverse demographics. At the same time, universities are faced with changes to funding models. Students attending the university today are not being adequately supported by their educational institutions, and as a result, students are not always able to succeed. While universities support many students, additional services need to be created to expand opportunities for all students.

Throughout part 2, advocacy is stressed in the sense that student success leaders and library workers can work together to better support students. The text asks readers to consider how libraries reflect the core values needed to design services for everyone. Collaboration between library employees and student success professionals is a good fit because both groups value equitable access to education, serve all students, and have a direct connection to the students from an interdisciplinary point of view without direct assessment. These collaborations fill a gap in current higher education structures by matching concern for student outcomes with information needs, leading to increased success for underprepared students.

In part 3, we outline the ways that academic library workers and academic success coordinators can collaborate effectively to meet the needs of underrepresented students. We advocate for a process of identifying shared information needs, defining success, and subsequently designing shared services in order to help meet student needs. In this process, cross-training helps in developing shared content expertise across campus. Generating shared content expertise on campus needs alone can lead to increased student success simply by educating others and creating a network of like-minded individuals to help foster success of students.

Part 4 introduces a model for continual improvement. By creating a culture of excellence around student support work, one can establish a regularly-paced analysis of new student needs and working to address them. This book by no means can address each and every student need; there are many. There will be new needs as this book gets published that we cannot address. As a result, having a plan to reevaluate, assess, and document the paths taken and what was learned, to identify which support structures helped, and which did not, is a part of a culture of excellence in serving students.

We hope that after reading this book, individuals will be able to more readily identify the barriers that limit undergraduate students' success in higher education. Using the book as a tool kit, they will be able to develop a plan for collaboration and partnership between library workers and student success administrators at any institution. Finally, readers will obtain deeper knowledge and understanding regarding the history of a student success and existing support structures within the university. This deeper knowledge includes the ability to understand the changing nature of higher education and how the system has perpetuated privileges, hegemonic knowledge, awareness, and skills.

CHAPTER ONE

Framing the Core Issue

Dr. Vincent Harding was a civil rights leader and historian who fought for change and social justice. In an interview with Krista Tippett on the radio show *On Being* (Tippett 2011), Harding called for the importance of working alongside or with those we serve. He suggested that it would behoove educators to consider standing in the darkness with the students who are in "so-called marginalized" communities. He stated:

> That would help them to see the possibilities for themselves. I've always felt that one of the things that we do badly in our educational process, especially working with so-called marginalized young people, is that we educate them to figure out how quickly they can get out of the darkness and get into some much more pleasant situation when what is needed again and again are more and more people like Gene who will stand in that darkness, who will not run away from those deeply hurt communities and will open up possibilities that other people can't see in any other way except seeing it through human beings who care about them. And if we teach young people to run away from the darkness rather than to open up the light in the darkness, to be the candles, the signposts, then we are doing great harm to them and the communities that they have come out of.

In this way, educators may be able to stand with students to acknowledge where they are and help them grapple with their situation and get to where they want to be. So much of what we explore in this book is about how to be near our students, to see them for who they are—including their skills and experiences—rather than trying to pull them out from where they are. Changing the students is not a sustainable solution; rather, educators must involve themselves in changing the landscape of higher education to make it more accessible to a wider variety of students. Educators, including library workers and advisors, commonly do serve as signposts. By working together across campus, it is possible to make broader and deeper connections for students and to help them maneuver through academia and receive great opportunities to shine.

What this book endeavors to do is to tell a story about how library workers can collaborate with advisors to create new services to meet these needs. This proposal is not looking to replace the hard work and exploration that students need to be able to do in college to succeed, graduate, and make fulfilling life plans. Instead, this text hopes to address the systems and real issues that our students face and that often present themselves as issues of retention.

The Context of Students' Lives

Each day, students engage in their campus communities to learn, work, and research. When students show up in higher education, they bring their backgrounds, experiences, struggles, families, and responsibilities. In other words, individual students bring their own particular contexts. Students' responsibilities and priorities may be complex, as some are increasingly in caretaker roles, caring for their own children, their parents, or other family members. Many are commuter students who have found a place in the library to study because they have no other place to go between classes. First-generation students may not be familiar with how the university system works. Some students have accessibility needs. They may run into barriers to success in a variety of other areas of their lives. Are contemporary U.S. colleges and universities prepared to support students from increasingly diverse points of access? If so, how?

The awareness of campus staff and faculty about student experiences varies. Sometimes staff and faculty learn of these struggles and barriers through conversations with students, in a coincidental way, while providing specific services. If students find that the staff or faculty are willing to listen or may be willing to help them or advocate for them, they may share more information about their lives. In each case, with each student, the issue may be different. In many situations, there may be very few or no services or responsible individuals on the college campus that can guide them to success. Students can have a difficult time overcoming barriers to graduate from the university or even to fit in and feel as if they belong there. They may also struggle with their undergraduate career when the real societal issues they may face are not resolved. How do universities communicate to all of their students that they belong, regardless of their backgrounds and experiences? How can we create a college experience for all students?

The individuals who work on the campus, and in particular library workers, or librarians (which will be used interchangeably to mean library workers), and advisors, are well poised to help serve these students in finding solutions, pathways, and opportunities to engage. This is due in part to their access to students through the roles of librarians and advisors. Librarians work to meet the information needs of students. Students who are struggling to feel they matter or to find meaning on campus may simply have information needs. They may be unaware of services that do exist. These students need information in order to succeed. For others, the services they need may not exist, and those services may need to be created. Those services would be support structures that help student performance.

All students, including those facing barriers, have myriad information needs, and library workers are in a unique position to see the full scope of the university. Library staff serves all students. That means their major doesn't matter to the library as a unique interdisciplinary academic department. Library workers will serve them regardless of their major, what type of learner they are, or what type of student they are. They can use the library whether they live in dorms on campus, commute from their parent's home over an hour away, or live in their car.

The Library as Interdisciplinary Student Success Hub

Students know that librarians are there to help them. Keeping in mind that two main factors that influence student success are a personal relationship with faculty and a peer group that will help students study, librarians can make a difference in serving as mentors or creating hubs for students to make connections. Why not highlight the resources of a library to amplify its use as an interdisciplinary hub for students? Libraries already are places that have what students need.

As library workers or advisors, it is possible to develop relationships with students. Throughout this book, we explore what might happen if we all stopped to learn more about our students, ask them how they are doing, and wait for their honest answers. Many students use the library, whether in person or online. These students fall into myriad categories; each student is unique, with unique concerns. We never know what is happening below the surface until we stop to find out.

Though many students face barriers, there is not always a fix for the students. Rather, the systems themselves, even the library services, need to be modified in order to allow students to flourish and thrive in higher education. In addition, librarians and advisors ought to avoid simple solutions that are sometimes disguised as innovations. Nothing can replace the path of establishing social networks and creating new collaborative services in a holistic manner, which provides authentic opportunities for all students.

Librarians can create networked hubs that provide access to resources. Students may need access to a variety of supports, from technologies to basic needs. By following in the tradition of meeting information needs through information access, libraries can become hubs of information creation services. Students with needs will come to these hubs if they are set up in such a way as to meet those needs. When a singular department or college (within a university) creates spaces like these it can be helpful to a student but when they're formed in an interdisciplinary space, not only does the capacity for service support increase but also students from every major come together. In informal spaces such as these, which can be both physical and online spaces, students can form strong connections with other students, find skills they can share with others, and learn new skills from peers in the space.

Seeing the library as an interdisciplinary hub for access can be a powerful change. Some library partnerships have made profound changes to students' lives. Librarians do not have to be responsible for the full delivery of all systems, but they can connect to others and bring them into the library, digitally and physically. Open Educational Resources (OER), in which students have zero cost for textbooks in their courses, is one example of a place where partnerships can bring expanded services. Librarians can partner with faculty and departments to deliver those services. Many librarians are working to partner with faculty in this way. Another less common example is childcare, where librarians don't need to deliver the services independently but can bring childcare facilities into the library.

Oregon State University's Valley Library identified a need for childcare services for their students and brought those services into the library; this is a great example of a successful partnership (Our Little Village Library n.d.). The campus childcare facilities provide up to three hours per day for parent-students so long as the parents remain in the library. At a drop-off child center, the parent-students are then able to complete their coursework without distraction, while their children obtain high-quality childcare. Since this service is free—already paid for with student fees—it is highly accessible and ought to be emulated in all campuses, especially those with high parent-student caregiving populations. If you'd like to look up more information on this, the National Survey of Student Engagement (NSSE) includes a question about caregiving for student populations.

This survey is delivered to freshmen and seniors enrolled in higher education institutions. The question that they ask of those populations is how many hours they spend weekly delivering care to dependents: "Providing care for dependents (children, parents, etc.)" (NSSE 2022). Though this question only asks about dependents, we cannot tell if this refers to other dependents, or children. This does give you an understanding of the caretaking responsibilities for students on average at your institution. More than 1,600 institutions participate in NSSE, but not all institutions have this data available. You can look up your institution and see if it participates. If not, you can always learn more about this student population through other means. While the NSSE website does not host the data collected from those surveys, that data are sometimes shared with or published publicly or by request at each institution.

The Changing Nature of Higher Education Student Populations

Student populations are changing rapidly. This book uses the terms "traditional" and "nontraditional" students. As outlined in chapter 2, the structures of higher education historically have best served students with high levels of social capital. "Traditional" has referred to students who are supported wholly or in major part by their families for tuition and housing, who are in the 18 to 24 age group, and who are coming directly from a high school experience that offers college preparation courses. Though this binary differentiation is not what we recommend, the terms are used in this book because of their historical context and also because of the research on this topic. The terms "traditional" and "nontraditional" should be fluid.

In different contexts, a nontraditional student may refer to one who does not live on campus, but commutes. A nontraditional student may be a parent. A nontraditional student could be someone older than 21 returning to college. Since the term "nontraditional" refers to many different groups with different needs, we recommend a strategy of being specific in identifying the exact population. In one's own institution, it is always better to address descriptors of the group being discussed. Nontraditional students may include, but are not limited to, the following groups (note: this list is not intended to be hierarchical): commuter students, distance education students, LGBTQIA+ students, immigrant students, international students, military students, Native American students, refugee students, students of color, students with disabilities, students over the age of 21, other underrepresented minorities, or veteran students. For instance, it's quite easy to see that commuting students have different needs from those who live on campus. Students who are parents of small children have different needs than those who do not have children. Even more specifically, single-parent students who commute to campus have many needs that differ from nonparent students who live on campus. Some of these needs are information needs, and some of these needs are services or even basic needs. Students who live on campus and who are 18 years old may also come from families who cannot financially support them. In all of these cases, students will have some shared information needs and other specific needs that will need to be met in order for them to be successful.

The definition of "nontraditional students" varies. Students above the age of 25 are referred to as post-traditional learners by the American Council on Education (Post-Traditional Learners n.d.). The National Center for Education Statistics defines nontraditional primarily by age as well. It notes on its website that there has been a significant amount of research into defining the qualities of nontraditional students (NCES n.d.). While this book proposes to adopt the phrase "at-promise" instead of "at-risk," we also find that "nontraditional students" is more common in some cases and that this language may also be exclusionary. Still, this term is useful when talking about the college or university structure supporting all students.

When discussing how to build a university structure that supports all students, we've used a particular definition throughout this book. Regardless of who the students are, how they pay, or where they come from, higher education must build equitable structures to support them all. Building those structures means changing the way some college or university systems are run or managed. Staff, faculty, and administrators, in order to make those changes, need a new way of thinking about students in these demographics. "Traditional," "nontraditional," or "at-risk" labels continue the dominant thinking of students as those needing to be fixed.

The term "at-risk," explored at greater length in chapter 3, is often used to refer to so-called marginalized groups who may be at risk of dropping out of the university. This book recommends dropping terms that include the deficit model of thinking. Dropping the phrase "at-risk" will help the way staff and faculty consider these students. One thinks of students differently simply by replacing the term with "at-promise." Rather than seeing these students as individuals who may drop out—at risk of not graduating—using the term "at-promise" may allow library workers to see the potential and ability in these students. How can we use this phrase to consider their experiences, their culture, their strengths, and their needs?

Words matter to students, and all of their experiences help guide them to success. When educators and advisors flip their language to refer to students as at-promise, they set the stage for success in our individual perceptions. By seeing students as those who can achieve, and by honoring them and their experiences, we become less inclined to try to fix the students. As educators, we can help them see how their prior experiences can help them succeed. The reason this is so important is that huge populations of students can be considered at-promise. They can be nontraditional students, caretakers of dependents, students from different racial or cultural backgrounds, people in the LGBTQIA+ identity landscape, or students who have disabilities. Our students have had a variety of experiences, and as educators, we can become adept at recognizing their skills.

Just to give you an example of how many students may fall into these categories, here are some important facts to explain how these students in these demographics may experience success or retention issues. In 2015, according to the National Center for Education Statistics (NCES), more than 75 percent of undergraduates were what is referred to as nontraditional students. Nontraditional students are defined as those who are over 25, work part-time or full-time, are married or divorced, or have kids (Labi 2015). According to Aisha Labi at the Lumina Foundation, "these students are especially vulnerable to the derailment of their educational trajectory" (2015). The six-year rate of college attainment differs for different populations. The National Student Clearinghouse Research Center (NSCRC) finds a variety of reasons for completion rates in higher education depending on the originating institution and other factors, including a discrepancy based on age. Race remains a factor impeding student success.

In the *Atlantic* article "Higher Education Should Lead the Efforts to Reverse Structural Racism" (2020), authors and experts Freeman A. Hrabowski III, Peter H. Henderson, and J. Kathleen Tracy make the case that colleges and higher education in general have a responsibility to tackle structural racism and assist students in achieving their goals and dreams. They write: "We in this field have an obligation to engage in this work, because we have become more central than ever to our students' American dreams. We hold out to our students the promises of an enriched life and social mobility, and yet we often fall short in providing these to all who arrive on our campuses."

Structural racism is evidenced by data that show demographic discrepancies in the six-year graduation rate. According to Hrabowski, Henderson, and Tracy (2020) the total average of students in higher education has a 60 percent six-year graduation rate, whereas Black students have a 40 percent six-year graduation rate. Later in the book, we discuss how the University of Maryland created new programs that attempted to increase retention and graduation among Black students. These included shared experiences and opportunities that library workers could re-create on their campuses. The programs ranged from community book reads to short courses on how to navigate college. Hrabowski, Henderson, and Tracy reiterate, "These provide students with a sense of belonging, agency, and efficacy, along with tools they need to be successful." Mattering and belonging are key issues for at-promise students, and this book touches on those issues throughout. The Meyerhoff Scholars Program at the University of Maryland–Baltimore County is highlighted as a successful program. The goal is to support students in obtaining advanced degrees. The program managers use collaboration across units to support students. Within the program, they work to ensure that students meet high expectations, to connect them to peers and others at the institution, and to bring the students into the research landscape. In sum, it is the responsibility of higher education institutions not only to set the stage for success but also to collaborate and create new programs to support students in new ways.

Consider the Responsibilities of Academic Libraries

Retention and success are key issues facing students, but what is the role of library staff and faculty in addressing this issue? How can the academic library meet the information needs of at-promise students? What have librarians and library staff already learned about student success? First and foremost, librarians have always cared about student success. At their core, libraries exist to serve the user. How can services be structured in a way to support students' needs in a way that helps them achieve their goals?

In existing academic library services, the library exists to meet users' information needs. Academic libraries often purchase books or databases based on user demand. Reference services meet users' point-of-need information questions. Library workers are uniquely poised, because of their information and technology skill sets and training, to facilitate content creation in the communities they serve. Facilitating knowledge creation in the library communities is an aspect of both new librarianship and participatory librarianship, researched primarily by R. David Lankes in the book *The Atlas of New Librarianship* (2011).

In this way, if we deliver the information to the user, and the user requests the information, how will our role morph? Academic library workers must have at their core the mission of student success: to retain students in higher education institutions. This will enable students to succeed in their goals.

Retention can be a complicated issue, as students drop out for many reasons. Some of them come back. Many of them have been hit by certain life circumstances that appear insurmountable and may think that no one else has had similar experiences. They may find that the college or university they attend cannot meet their needs. They may feel hesitant to reach out for the services that can be provided to help them succeed. Many of these services exist, and there are many opportunities for library workers, advisors, and educators to work together and create solid foundations for these students so that they may succeed in their college education and beyond.

Consider the Place of Darkness

As you continue in this book, it will help to think about any barriers you may have encountered in higher education, or barriers you know others have run into. If none come to mind for higher education, any barrier or obstacle will work. Of course, as adults with many life experiences it is easy to look back and see obstacles or barriers as opportunities. However, most of us have experienced plenty of obstacles that felt insurmountable at the time. Consider that precise moment when you felt stuck. What was it that helped you get beyond the obstacle, if you did? Or is it something you are still struggling to overcome? What helped you, and what would help you? Often, there are systems that are barriers, and while the systems may be there for a reason, they may also keep out many legitimate requests. Was the answer truly something that came from within you? Did someone else help you? Was change an improvement or an answer you can bring about within yourself, or are there external situational obstacles that can be modified or changed to remove those barriers?

Another way to look at it would be to think about any time you have ever had a moment where you wondered why things exist the way that they are, such as the design or orientation of a bathroom, or why crosswalks are designed the way they are. Or have you ever wondered if there was a service for individuals in specific situations? Did you find healing in overcoming a particular challenge? Barriers can sometimes present as punishment. More often than not, when you did succeed, it was because someone lent a hand or a change was made. The question posed to libraries and universities today is the same. How can we offer services that will help all students succeed? This is the question to keep in mind as you explore within this book.

Student success may mean different things to each individual. Students have their own goals, and success may be meeting those goals. Sometimes, the goals may be about how to improve their lives while remaining a part of their own communities. How can higher education best support students to both continue to be a part of the community where they are from and to obtain a degree and job success? In some cases, it may mean staying in their home community while obtaining education, though it may not always mean this. For some students, success means being able to think of themselves as a college graduate. Success may mean that the students are able to graduate, then continue on to do the kinds of work they want to do. The nature of success is individualistic. Consider how to adjust the agenda of the university to become more equitable for students, all of whom have individualized goals and run into unique barriers.

Libraries and the workers within them have a responsibility to help students achieve their goals. By understanding that the students know where they want to go, reaching them where they are, and recognizing they have the skills and experiences to reach those goals, we can learn more about them and support them to obtain success. Library workers have essential information skills that can be used to connect with other educators and student success professionals on college campuses to build new programs and support all students. These are performance metrics—all students need support structures, opportunities and programs to succeed. Through collaboration, library workers, student success professionals, and other campus leaders can build these structures.

Benefits Hub Example

Throughout this book we highlight many partnerships that have brought about student success as inspiration and to assist with generating creative ideas to pursue. The University of Washington–Bothell Benefits Hub is located in the Activities and Recreation Center on campus. Though this is not a partnership with an academic library, the Benefits Hub partnership is an idea that could be replicated on other college campuses and that would involve a library and other services. This partnership is between the University of Washington–Bothell and United Way of King County. Most importantly, this partnership shows how many resources can be applied to maintain successful partnerships.

This Benefits Hub offers resources to assist students in reaching their full potential. The campus took the ideas about what students really need the most, identified the true barriers, and set about creating this space. There are resource coaches that help students learn more and obtain training in key areas, based on the barriers they identified. These include training on financial literacy, credit, and financial planning; support in signing up for resource programs like SNAP or FAFSA; and learning about other networked campus providers such as food banks.

Hodara, Riggs, and Brey (2021), researchers from the education nonprofit Education Northwest, report on research and grant partnerships, including the benefits hubs. Their report, "Early Findings from ECMC Foundation's Basic Needs Initiative," focuses on how to meet the basic needs of college students. In a recent study, 60 percent of college students from over 50 colleges and 28 different states report that they have basic needs insecurity. Benefits Hubs, like the one in Bothell, "provide housing, food, and financial supports." Through the partnership and the grant, "Benefits Hubs campuses will receive staffing support from UWKC and participate in a learning cohort with other Benefits Hub campus champions." This partnership is the best kind—working to identify barriers and simultaneously educate students while connecting them to solutions.

Though through this partnership, grant funds are fueling the services, developing mechanisms for ongoing sustenance is important. The United Way is providing staffing resources, and the University of Washington–Bothell provides staff and space. After the grant period ends, it will be important to collect data and decide how to sustain this partnership. In this way, collecting assessment and impact data can help make the argument for obtaining long-term resources. In the next chapter, we will review information about assessment and evaluation and how this works into the revision process.

References

Hodara, Michelle, Sam Riggs, and Libbie Brey. 2021. "Early Findings from ECMC Foundation's Basic Needs Initiative." Education Northwest. https:// educationnorthwest.org/sites/default/files/ecmc-bni-evaluation-brief.pdf.

Hrabowski, Freeman A., III, Peter H. Henderson, and J. Kathleen Tracy. 2020, October 24. "Higher Education Should Lead the Efforts to Reverse Structural Racism." *The Atlantic.* https://www.theatlantic.com/ideas/archive /2020/10/higher-education-structural-racism/616754.

Labi, Aisha. 2015. "Placing Student Success at the Center of State Higher Education Finance Policy." Lumina Issue Papers. https://www.luminafoundation .org/files/resources/labi-student-success-at-the-center.pdf.

Lankes, R. David. 2011. *The Atlas of New Librarianship.* Cambridge, MA: MIT Press.

NCES (National Center on Education Statistics). n.d. "Definitions and Data." Accessed March 22, 2022. https://nces.ed.gov/pubs/web/97578e.asp.

NSSE. 2022. "NSSE Survey Instruments." Indiana University. https://nsse.indiana .edu/nsse/survey-instruments/index.html.

"Our Little Village Library." n.d. Oregon State University. Accessed March 22, 2022. https://familyresources.oregonstate.edu/olv-library.

"Post-Traditional Learners." n.d. American Council on Education. Accessed March 22, 2022. https://www.acenet.edu/Research-Insights/Pages/Student -Support/Post-Traditional-Learners.aspx.

Tippett, Krista. 2011. "Vincent Harding: Is America Possible?" On Being. https:// onbeing.org/programs/vincent-harding-is-america-possible.

PART 1

Background of Student Success

CHAPTER TWO

The History of Student Success

Historical Practice as It Continues to Impact Contemporary Access

The purpose of this book is to outline why and how to build new services for both existing and emerging populations enrolling in universities. Campus administrators throughout the history of higher education in the United States have restricted access to services and admission based on many demographic factors. Racially motivated exclusion from universities and discrimination through the denial of resources constitute just one dimension of a system founded to privilege access for white, landed families in the United States. Applying a racial lens to the history of higher education yields a cohesive narrative that describes access to higher education in social, economic, and political terms (Harper, Patton, and Wooden 2009). In keeping with the scope of the book, this chapter outlines the historical barriers to success that students of color have suffered as a direct impact of white supremacy in higher education. With the goal of providing a snapshot of historical context to understand access issues in higher education in the United States, this history of student success will spotlight one dimension of student identity, focusing on narratives that stem from a racial lens. The history of higher education illuminates the struggle for underrepresented populations to emerge and thrive in a system that was made deliberately to disadvantage similar populations throughout time.

The authors advocate working for inclusion across all identities in student populations. This work primarily draws from undergraduate experiences at public universities in the United States. International schools, private colleges, for-profit colleges, community colleges, junior colleges, and vocational schools are a limited focus of research and discussion, though some theory and history presented in this account may inform practice at these institutions. Lessons learned through this work will benefit individuals in all colleges and universities in that they will help readers understand how access limitations have impeded student success. Ultimately, we must provide more services to help a wide variety of individuals thrive in higher education.

The founding and the subsequent growth of the United States and the U.S. higher education industry largely benefited landed white colonists who became white U.S. citizens. In their article "Toward a Critical Race Theory," Ladson-Billings and Tate (1995) argue that "the intersection of race and property creates an analytic tool through which we can understand social (and, consequently, school) inequity" (p. 48). They note that "slavery linked the privilege of Whites to the subordination of Blacks through a legal regime that attempted the conversion of Blacks into objects of property" (p. 58)." (Ladson-Billings and Tate 1995). Leading up to Reconstruction, following the U.S. Civil War, Indigenous, Black, Chinese, and Mexican workers faced interpersonal exclusion, systemic discrimination, or even death while pursuing education and university experiences. As time moved on, discrimination within the university and the application process for higher education became more complex in overt and covert ways of diminishing the dignity of populations of color.

From the moment the first colonial university was founded, there have been significant events that systematically hindered access to American higher education, the impact of which reverberated throughout history and continued to exacerbate an achievement gap among white students and students of color.

Student affairs preparation programs are in varying stages of incorporating a history of college student services that overviews the interplay of historical, national campus events with privilege and power. In order to understand structural racism and other disenfranchising phenomena in higher education, student affairs personnel must understand key historical events and their impact on access. The American College Personnel Association (ACPA) and the National Association of Student Personnel Administrators (NASPA) work together to set industry standards in student affairs and higher education. The organizations met in 2010 to create the Joint Task Force on Professional Competencies and Standards. They identified 10 areas of competence for preparation programs, which include a "values, philosophy, and history" (VPH) area of recommendations.

In 2015, a joint publication between the ACPA and NASPA organizations offered revisions to the output of the 2010 Joint Task Force on Professional Competencies and Standards. The 2015 updates explicitly reference social justice and inclusion and recommend that practitioners move away from "an awareness of diversity"—that is, familiarity with social justice literature—to "a more active orientation" (Johnson Eanes et al. 2015) that reflects diversity, equity, and inclusion. For example, practitioners ought to move from an intellectual regard for diversity to practices like equitably redistributing resources. Obviously, student affairs preparation programs across the United States are young in their development to provide adequate information on the intersection of power, privilege, and access shaping higher education.

Many preparation programs are developing their diversity, equity, and inclusion learning outcomes for their history course. It is necessary to understand the history of higher education from its inception as it leads up to contemporary practice. As many higher education history textbooks begin, Harvard happened to the United States. Higher education preparation programs in the United States vary throughout the country. In many accounts from books and textbooks, histories of American higher education describe an alleged big bang of scholarly activity where there was once a supposed intellectual and physical blank slate. White imperialism and its failure to consider student success in nonwhite populations are embedded in these first moments of the conception of American higher education, thereby making the founding itself exclusionary.

Founding of American Higher Education: Religious and Capitalist Influences

The land on which Harvard now stands was not a blank slate. When the Massachusetts Bay Colony reached the land that would come to be known as Cambridge, they fought the Pequot people for control of the land. *Ebony & Ivy: Race, Slavery, and the Troubled History of America's University* (Wilder 2013) describes the origins of higher education in the United States as intertwined with Black slavery and Native American genocide. As white colonists traded the first African people into the colonies in 1619, slave owners trained slaves in professions such as masonry and carpentry. With these skills, slaves built the structures that would become the first buildings of the first campuses. Harvard was established in 1636 to spread Protestantism, to assimilate Native populations, and to prepare the sons of land and property owners. In *New England's First Fruits*, a 1643 book published in London as a public relations response to criticism that there was not enough evangelism happening in New England, the authors describe the contemporary ethos toward Natives, stating that "Harvard offered free education to Indians and encouraged Englishe students to learn Algonquian" and "Native students also dressed in English clothese, marking their cultural submission. The English sought to correct Indians appears speech and beliefs." Harvard investors further encouraged Native assimilation. "In New England and Virginia, the English brought Indian children into schools to learn the ways of the Christian God and to swear loyalty to English and their government" (*New England's First Fruits* 1643). According to archives at the Peabody Museum, the first brick building on Harvard's campus was known as "the Harvard Indian College, and by 1655, five native students attended the school" (Elefante and

Goldsmith 2015). In the interest of attracting donors to the colonies, colonists cleared the lands of Indigenous people who resisted a cultural genocide.

The majority of the individuals in the Pequot tribes engaged in attrition warfare with the Narragansett. In the area that would become Cambridge, "the evangelism of the Protestant groups attracted donors, although in time the colonial colleges' devotion to such educational plans waned (the Church)" (Thelin et al. 2019). Colonists sold Pequot and Narragansett survivors into slavery or assimilated them into colonist culture and positioned them against their former tribespeople. When Harvard first opened, the school only admitted Christian men. As the institution expanded its physical reach coupled with its hegemonic privileging of white, landed, students local colonizers pushed Native communities farther away from their land, exacerbating Native cultural genocide. In addition to decimating Native populations from what would become Cambridge, "only white Christian males were allowed to matriculate. Women and African-Americans were denied participation by statute and custom" (Thelin et al. 2019). However, Native Americans were constrained to enroll but only to serve the campus and surrounding communities in a missionary capacity (Thelin et al. 2019). Similarly, nine other colonial colleges saw the foundation of their schools and admission processes based on religion.

Religious interests from multiple faiths ushered along Harvard's progress in becoming a physical place. The authors of *New England's First Fruits* noted that "after God had carried us safe to New-England, and wee had builded our houses, provided necessaries for our livelihood. . . . One of the next things we longed for, and looked after was to advance Learning and perpetuate it to Posterity; dreading to leave an illiterate Ministry to the Churches" (*New England's First Fruits* 1643). The authors go on to state that Mr. Harvard, "a godly gentleman and a lover of learning, gave one-half of his estate (it being in all about £1,700) towards the erecting of a Colledge" (*New England's First Fruits* 1643). However, as time and institutions evolved, economic interests were often a weightier stakeholder. For example, Reverend Blair, a ranking official of the Church of England in Virginia, emphasized the value of a college in training ministers to save colonial souls. Sir Edward Seymour, a treasury official and Blair's contemporary responded, "Souls!" and went on to exclaim, "Damn your soul, Make tobacco!" Higher education served profit-driven goals over educational goals from its inception.

Capitalism Drives the Interests of Limiting Access

Alongside the imperialism of higher education as a means to further religious interests, higher education expansion has been driven by elite economic interests since its inception. Instead of an education-driven or knowledge-driven mission and vision, higher education demonstrates a history of entrenching capitalism and widening class gaps that persists today. Inequity in higher education has been intrinsic since its foundation. John Locke's 1693 work *Some Thoughts Concerning Education* reflected his views on education. Locke remarked that the purpose of higher education was indeed to perpetuate inequities. He wrote that education should be focused on "educating the upper class boys to be moral, rationally-thinking, and reflecting." Higher education histories describe the operational mission and vision of campus as being borrowed philosophically from the cultures of European education. Grooming new slaveholders would occupy higher education goals until the U.S. Civil War in 1861. "College life was designed as a system for controlling the often exuberant (white) youth and for inculcating discipline, morals and character. Each student was to attend the lectures and tutorials, obey the rules, and avoid the company of base people" (Cohen and Kisker 2010, p. 27). Higher education served as a weapon of war abroad as well as at home.

These American colleges emerged in concert with "Europeans nations' attempts to seize territories. . . . European power deployed colleges to help defend and regulate the African slave trade to fund these efforts" (Wilder 2013, p. 9). Colonies further restricted the rights of nonwhite populations. During the earliest years of U.S. history, African Americans were prohibited from learning to read or write (Institute for Higher Education Policy 2010). For example, legislation reduced into one the several acts concerning slaves, "free negroes and mulattoes, and for other purposes . . . forbidding them to preach, carry weapons, sell alcohol, or exert freedom of speech or of the press," among other things. Legislators revised Virginia's General Assembly Chapter XXII Act to read "if any person shall hereafter write, print, or cause to be written or printed, any book, pamphlet or other writing, advising personals of colour," the individual would meet severe punishment, up to and including death (Schwarz 1988).

War Shapes Access to Higher Education: Civil War through World War II

Black Americans had to break through slavery's restriction on accessing universities as well as their lack of formal preparation for university study. Several approaches called for an end to slavery, but the road to inclusion and equity in higher education would continue to be fraught with obstacles. In some key areas, however, policies tried to slowly effect equity. An act in one state created paperwork hurdles to make slaveholding inconvenient. In 1780, the General Assembly of Pennsylvania established an Act for the Gradual Abolition of Slavery, which called for slave owners to register their enslaved individuals each year. Education for slaves was met with hostility and physical abuse. After Nat Turner's revolt in 1831, Southern states passed laws prohibiting the teaching of reading and writing to slaves. Because of this,

Abolitionists focused on teaching these skills to slaves. Abolitionists, however, did not approach accessing teaching and learning with slaves on a peer-to-peer level. Accounts from the time period reflect teaching skills to freed Blacks in order to either expatriate them, try to assimilate or "tame them," or socialize them from slave to "human." Abolitionists founded Liberia College (University of Liberia) located in Monrovia, Liberia, with the goal of strengthening financial ties to Africa. Liberia College created a "remarkably close copy of common schools, academies, and colleges on American's eastern seaboard" (Livingston 1976, p. 246). Though the establishment of Liberia College (1816–1841) provided a new opportunity to freed slaves, the initiative avoided systemic change in slavery law. The founders organized around the idea that if no one wanted Black people to be free in the United States, maybe there could be a place for people in Liberia. As the United States moved into civil unrest, a looming war impacted higher education, because fewer men were available to attend higher education. Systems had to change. Higher education in the South strained as students left the Southern institutions for the Civil War. "The death of thousands of young southern men meant that for schools to survive they needed to expand beyond teaching planter's sons. In order to attract more practically minded and economically diverse students, many southern institutions implemented elective systems that provided more curricular choices by adding engineering and scientific programs and by doing so they created the South's first authentic Universities" (Frost 2013, p. 262). Student demographics changed to reflect veterans returning injured. In some cases, institutions served as hospitals for veterans in one part of campus, and students enrolled as their health was restored. Other institutions served as a temporary home for freed slaves, or as stables for horses. Still other institutions were physically broken down and used as fuel for fire to keep soldiers warm.

Part of rebuilding the South after the Civil War involved legislation to increase the number of skilled professionals in the agricultural and mechanical fields. This legislation came in the form of the Morrill Act of 1862; however, institutional discrimination persisted. This act granted "land to each state for the purpose of dedicated higher ed buildings" with the intent to provide facilities for students to study "forestry, agriculture, and mechanics" (Frost 2013). Land grants "proved to be the major stimulus for the founding of state colleges occupational utility" (Frost 2013), which preserved colleges focusing on "liberal and practical education of the industrial classes in the pursuits and professions of life" (July 2, 1862, ch. 130, §1, 12 Stat. 503). While the act does not specifically delegate funds to support populations of color, it did change the amount of access to higher education institutions.

At the same time in history, another underrepresented population breaks through to enrollment. Thirty years after the Morrill Acts, individuals of Chinese descent began to be admitted to universities. As a result of the founding of the Morrill Act of 1862, and after Yung Wing became the first

Chinese person to graduate Yale in 1854, the Chinese Educational Mission sent Chinese citizens to study in the United States. Wing then led these groups. Wing "supervised groups of young Chinese to the United States to study Western science and engineering." Yung Wing faced challenges working to introduce "new science of the west in China due to scholars who could not write Chinese and Chinese scholars who could not understand the language of the original work and of the foreign translation" (Harris 1994, p. 103). Wing supported 120 students through their educational route. Although the mission was proceeding, the Naturalization Act of 1870 deemed all Chinese people living and working in the United States to be ineligible for citizenship. Chinese rights to own land and rights to enter certain professions dissolved. Further exclusion acts would follow through the start of the new century (Xiao 2015). The U.S. government granted exceptions to people of "African descent" in light of the 14th Amendment.

While the 13th Amendment brought slavery to an end, the 14th Amendment ensured legal protections, and the 15th established voting rights for all folks of color (Smithsonian American Art Museum 2014), any movement toward achieving equity in higher education would continue to be slow. Even with the enactment of the Morrill Act of 1862, an act that established a parcel of land in each state to be dedicated to housing a university (7 U.S.C. 301 et seq.), the federal government was unable to gain cooperation from the Southern states in the provision of land-grant support to the "Negro" institutions. To overcome this problem, a second Morrill Act was passed in 1890 specifically to support the so-called Negro land-grant institutions. The 1890 Act stated that no appropriations would go to states that denied admissions to the colleges on the basis of race unless they set up separate but equal facilities. Thus the Negro land-grant institutions are referred to today as the "1890 Institutions." Those Southern States that did not have Negro institutions by 1890 each established one later under this act. The second Morrill Act (26 Stat. 417, 7 U.S.C. § 321 et seq.) initiated regular appropriations to support land-grant colleges, which came to include 17 predominantly African American colleges (Edelson 2015) and 30 American Indian (Association of Public and Land-Grant Universities 2012) colleges. The act prohibited racial discrimination in the South, and the sheer need for students to attend to keep the universities funded and functioning allowed interracial enrollment. This led to an influx of poor whites and Black students who sustained the rebuilding of universities by supplying additional funding sources. However, the U.S. Supreme Court's 1896 decision in *Plessy v. Ferguson* impacted institutions of higher education, because all education entities needed thereafter to provide separate but equal facilities for white students and students of color.

The separate but equal doctrine would impact higher education formally when it was overturned in 1954 in *Brown v. Board of Education of Topeka*. This decision would continue to impact higher education through the present day, though one of the first impacts of *Plessy* in higher education could be felt in the increase of "historically Black colleges." As whites moved west, they crushed Indigenous populations, and though Native Americans attended the United States' first university, Reconstruction-era higher education reflected small Indigenous enrollment. Chinese workers moved into higher education, and China sent students to the United States until the Chinese Exclusion Laws took effect (Shirley 2018).

As veterans returned from WWI, "most veterans of the American Expeditionary Force received $60, a new set of clothes, a train ticket home, and the opportunity to purchase a modest life insurance policy" (Gelber 2005, p. 161). The Federal Board for Vocational Education (FBVE) established two sections to direct aid to the returning soldiers. Section 2 helped students rehabilitate to another profession if they were unable to return to their pre-war vocation. Students enrolled in Section 3 gave "free instruction but no stipend to veterans with minor disabilities" p. 163 (Gelber 2005). Enrollment and completion of the FBVE retraining courses would allow veterans to receive assistance with their job searches. Although the support extended to all veterans, the FBVE advisors discriminated against Mexican, Asian, and Black veterans. FBVE advisors could deny anyone due to the Sections 2 and 3's vague guidelines for granting support. Intelligence tests further informed FBVE's discrimination. Tests, which were designed to test cultural background and not capacity, ability, or aptitude, showed that "the average mental age of soldiers was only 13 and that between 30 and 50 percent of white men, and 80 and 90 percent of black men, were technically 'moronic'" (Gelber 2005, p. 168). Advisors deemed soldiers in these categories inherently unable to absorb education or training, and they were placed in lower-wage jobs suitable in skill for their perceived intelligence.

Higher education enrollment saw shifts in attitude toward advanced study. Job creation fell as the country moved into the Great Depression. A misconception about the Great Depression is that people fled to enroll in higher education as a result of fewer employment opportunities (Schrecker 2020). Many would-be prospective students could not afford shoes (United States 1933), let alone tuition, and they wrote to First Lady Eleanor Roosevelt to ask her to provide. "The young bore a disproportionate burden of poverty" (Samuel et al. 2021). The Relief Census of 1933 found that people of color, specifically Blacks, represented up to three times the number of whites receiving relief. Enrollment in colleges dipped because people in the United States were recovering from the stock market crash. Furthermore, relief receivers' peers did not believe they ought to attend college at all given their class station, as "could be seen among the elitist segment of college youth who argued that only the affluent should attend college" (Reiman 1993, p. 9).

The rush to out-develop (Thompson 2019) fascist countries led to the implementation of the Servicemen's Readjustment Act of 1944, which established benefits for veterans. GI Benefits following World War II relieved some of the strain on people hoping to attend college. Under the act, approximately 2,300,000 attended colleges and universities, 3,500,000 received school training, and 3,400,000 received on-the-job training (U.S. Congress 1956). The number of degrees awarded in the United States more than doubled as veterans enrolled. Overall, in historical accounts, the education portion of the GI Bill in World War II is portrayed as democratizing higher education in the United States (Trow 2005), moving the institutions from elitist to available for prospective students across social class. However, the opportunities that the Servicemen's Readjustment Act of 1944 offered were not available evenly across all veteran demographics (U.S. Congress 1956) because *Plessy v. Ferguson* legislation sanctioned white Southern politicians to police the "distribution of benefits under the GI Bill to uphold their segregationist beliefs" (Thompson 2019). Black servicemen often applied for GI benefits with fragmented K–12 education. They were often denied admission due to the high volume of students attempting to access historically Black universities (HBCUs) and other Southern universities. Schools often could not accommodate the large numbers of veteran prospective students. And often Southern schools did not benefit from government support and aid at a level comparable to Northern colleges and universities.

Policy Increases Access to Higher Education

Perhaps the most profound legal decision to force higher education practices to change from exclusionary to inclusive of all individuals is found in *Brown v. Board of Education* (1954). The decision changed where the colleges students decided to enroll in were located and the student demographics at each college. While it did not change the interpersonal discrimination students of color experienced on campuses, it did make illegal the provision of separate but equal services. Prior to *Brown v. Board* overturning *Plessy v. Ferguson*, most students of color attended HBCUs during their undergraduate experience. As a result of the change (Egerton 1974), more students of color enrolled in predominantly white institutions (PWIs). As Harvey, Harvey, and King noted in their article, "The Impact of the Brown v. Board of Education Decision on Postsecondary Participation of African Americans" (2004), PWIs, "characterized themselves as fair-minded," and thought of universities as "thoughtful settings where appropriately qualified students and professors engaged in the search for truth and the pursuit of knowledge" (p. 329). However, before *Brown v. Board*, "it was not necessarily the depth of one's intellect that was the appropriate qualification to gain entry into the academy, but the color of one's skin" (Harvey, Harvey, and King 2004, p. 329). *Brown v. Board* has had a lasting impact. Enrollment trends reflected "18- to 24-year-olds increased from 35 percent in 2000 to 41 percent in

2018. In 2018, the college enrollment rate was higher for 18- to 24-year-olds who were Asian (59 percent) than for 18- to 24-year-olds who were White (42 percent), Black (37 percent), and Hispanic (36 percent)" (U.S. Department of Education 2020a).

The following decade saw more access to higher education for more students of color as a result of both student-led movements and changing legislation. Students and legislation impacted higher education in the United States. Students protested apartheid, the Vietnam War, and the dearth of gay and lesbian civil rights. In these protests, students shaped higher education to meet their needs. This included founding the first ethnic studies programs (College of Ethnic Studies n.d.), despite condescension from university administrators, who advocated a "time-out" for protestors ("Timeline" 2016). The emergence of student-led protests and the resulting institutionalization of the lived experience of students of color in ethnic studies further cracked open access to a diversity of student demographics.

Standardized testing in college entrance exams sparked intense debates on whether the SAT and CEEB tests gave a clear picture of a students' readiness for college or perpetuated racial bias and stereotypes (Hanford 1976). In loco parentis, or the philosophy that higher education served students just as parents might, disintegrated as more students exercised their agency and as the number of students having a traditional college experience decreased. Whose parents and whose expectations were university administrators serving? (Lee 2011). Individual states, among them California, enacted policies to respond to a change, such as the 1960 Masterplan for Higher Education. This policy created a system that "combined exceptional quality with broad access for students" (California 1960). The policy envisioned higher education in California as a single continuum of educational opportunity, from small private colleges to large public universities. As a part of the War on Poverty, The Education Opportunity Act of 1964, an "unprecedented increase in federal spending on college student support reflecting a mixture of grant, loan and work-study programs" (Long 2013), established Upward Bound. This program "continues to serve high school students from low-income families and high school students from families in which neither parent holds a bachelor's degree" with the goal of increasing the "rate at which participants complete secondary education and enroll in and graduate from institutions of postsecondary education" (U.S. Department of Education 2020b). Following the Education Opportunity Act of 1964, President Lyndon B. Johnson signed the Civil Rights Act of 1964 (Harper, Patton, and Wooden 2009). Title VI of the Act provided that "no person in the United States, on the grounds of race, color, or national origin, be excluded from participation in, or the benefits of, or be subjected to discrimination under any program or activity receiving federal financial assistance" (Malaney 1987, 17). Title VI also restricted the distribution of federal funds to segregated schools. In 1965, U.S. president Lyndon B. Johnson officially brought John F. Kennedy's vision to fruition with the signing of Executive Order 11246, which required federal contractors to increase the number of minority employees as an "affirmative step" toward remedying years of exclusion for minority workers in those firms; affirmative action was systematically enacted that year (United States 1990). The 1965 Higher Education Act provided national assistance to schools meeting a set of criteria to meaningfully recruit and retain communities of color through robust and developmentally tailored scholarships and grants (Rosehan 1967).

For example, Special Services for Disadvantaged Students, which later became Student Support Services, was launched in 1968, and the federally funded programs encouraged access to higher education for low-income students (United States 1990). The act developed college preparatory classes to increase the number of students who may have come from parts of the country in which they did not have access to coursework in high school that prepared them for college-level study. Title III and Title IV of the same act increased support to minority-serving institutions (MSIs), including historically Black colleges and universities (HBCUs), predominantly Black institutions (PBIs), Hispanic-serving institutions (HSIs), Tribal colleges or universities (TCUs), Native American or non-Tribal institutions (NANTI), Alaska Native or Native Hawaii–serving institutions (ANNHI), and Asian American and Native American Pacific Islander–serving institutions (AANAPISI) (U.S. Department of Education n.d.). As access to higher education increased through the civil rights movement, the United States entered a litigious era in which policy designed to increase student diversity faced challenges.

The Pell Grant, officially known as the Basic Educational Opportunity Grant (BEOG), was established in 1972 and in 1973–1974 began funding students earning their first bachelor's or associate's degree who demonstrated financial need. Students benefiting from the Pell Grant can focus more on school because they do not have to also work to cover all education costs while attending classes (Klebs 2020). Pell Grant students are more likely to be students of color, first generation, or low income. The Supreme Court's 1978 ruling on Allan Bakke's admission to the medical school at the University of California–Davis (Regents of the University of California v. Allan Bakke 1978) upheld the use of race in admissions in principle but concluded that the medical school's practice of reserving 16 of its 100 admission slots for Black, Hispanic, Native American, and Asian American applicants was tantamount to a quota system that discriminated against whites (Gutiérrez 2013). Grutter v. Bollinger (2003) upheld the use of affirmative action in law school admissions, meaning that campus admissions can affirmatively admit students on the basis of race. In the following years, several challenges tried to overturn affirmative action but did not succeed.

Issues of access in higher education are increasingly intersectional. Currently, a prevailing issue in terms of access to higher education calls for the reexamination of affirmative action's racial focus because the practice misses student populations—for example, strivers—that are struggling for access. Strivers are an emerging student population that, while high achieving, come from support systems with limited economic support for college and may also come from depressed educational environments where they have little access to college preparation courses. The effect can be seen in trends such as students excelling in the highest-level courses available at their high school but testing much lower than other first-year admits on the SAT (Steinberg 1999). However, a common characteristic of strivers is that they trend toward concealing class status as a means to survive, and they distance themselves from their families of origin as a way to more deeply assimilate into university cultures. Strivers are further caught in an interstitial borderlands (Morton 2021), where they code switch to thrive, network, and function in academic settings but must retain their family of origin's cultural patterns in order to avoid alienation.

In the following chapters are our recommendations for practice, given the history of systemic access restrictions. We call for exploring bias in instructors and student success practitioners who may privilege only a narrow range of communication styles. We are calling for increasing segmentation in serving underrepresented student populations to find trends in attrition among students who fit a striver description. We advocate for basic needs providers to address the multiple and intersecting needs for retention presented by students. Strivers need increased support in building the cultural capital to excel in business worlds and cultures that they did not grow up with. Finally, we advocate for higher education to move from a culture of developing an individual to developing an ecology of families so that strivers don't have to drop their family's culture in favor of succeeding in a higher education environment.

References

Act of July 2, 1862 (Morrill Act), Public Law 37-108, Which Established Land Grant Colleges, 07/02/1862. n.d. Enrolled Acts and Resolutions of Congress, 1789–1996. Record Group 11. General Records of the United States Government. National Archives.

Association of Public and Land-Grant Universities. 2012. "The Land-Grant Tradition: 150 Years of Learning, Discovery and Engagement." https://www.aplu.org/library/the-land-grant-tradition/file.

California. Liaison Committee of the Regents of the University of California and the State Board of Education. 1960. *A Master Plan for Higher Education in California, 1960–1975*. Sacramento: Assembly of the State of California.

Cohen, A., and C. Kisker. 2010. *The Shaping of American Higher Education: Emergence and Growth of the Contemporary System*. San Francisco, CA: Jossey-Bass.

College of Ethnic Studies. n.d. "History." Accessed May 4, 2021. https://ethnicstudies.sfsu.edu/history.

Edelson, D. 2015, February 18. "Council of 1890s Institutions." Association of Public and Land-Grant Universities. https://www.aplu.org/members/councils/1890-universities/council-of-1890s-institutions.html.

Egerton, J. 1974. "Adams v. Richardson: Can Separate Be Equal?" *Change* 6 (10): 29–36.

Elefante, Valerie, and Annie M. Goldsmith. 2015, November 12. "Native Americans at Harvard." *Harvard Crimson*. https://www.thecrimson.com/article/2015/11/12/na-diversity-feature/.

Frost, D. 2013. Review of *Reconstructing the Campus: Higher Education and the American Civil War*, by Michael David Cohen. *Register of the Kentucky Historical Society* 111, no. 2 (Spring): 261–63.

Gelber, Scott. 2005. "A 'Hard-Boiled Order': The Reeducation of Disabled WWI Veterans in New York City." *Journal of Social History* 1 (39): 161–80.

General Assembly of Pennsylvania. 1780. "An Act for the Gradual Abolition of Slavery." Avalon Project: Documents in Law, History and Diplomacy. https://avalon.law.yale.edu/18th_century/pennst01.asp.

Grutter v. Bollinger. 2003. 539 U.S. 306.

Gutiérrez, R. 2013. "Higher Education and Equity: Historical Narratives, Contemporary Debates." *Diversity and Democracy* 16, no. 2 (Spring): 4–7.

Hanford, G. 1976. *Minority Programs and Activities of the College Entrance Examination Board: A Critical Review and Brief Look Ahead*. Princeton, NJ: College Entrance Examination Board.

Harper, S. R., L. D. Patton, and O. S. Wooden. 2009. "Access and Equity for African American Students in Higher Education: A Critical Race Historical Analysis of Policy Efforts." *Journal of Higher Education* 80 (4): 389–414. https://doi.org/10.1080/00221546.2009.11779022.

Harris, P. 1994. "A Checkered Life: Yung Wing's American Education." *American Journal of Chinese Studies* 2, no. 1 (April): 87–107.

Harvey, W., Adia M. Harvey, and M. King. 2004. "The Impact of the Brown v. Board of Education Decision on Postsecondary Participation of African Americans." *Journal of Negro Education* 73 (3): 328–40. https://doi.org/10.2307/4129615.

Institute for Higher Education Policy. 2010. "A Snapshot of African Americans in Higher Education." https://files.eric.ed.gov/fulltext/ED521322.pdf.

Johnson Eanes, B., P. A. Perillo, T. Fechter, S. Gordon, S. Harper, P. Havice, J. L. Hoffman, et al. 2015. *Professional Competency Areas for Student Affairs*. https://www.naspa.org/images/uploads/main/ACPA_NASPA_Professional_Competencies_FINAL.pdf.

Klebs, Shelbe. 2020, July 20. "Why We Should Double the Pell Grant." Third Way. https://www.thirdway.org/memo/why-we-should-double-the-pell-grant.

Ladson-Billings, G., and W. F. Tate. 1995. "Toward a Critical Race Theory of Education." *Teachers College Record* 97 (1): 47–68.

Lee, P. 2011. "The Curious Life of In Loco Parentis at American Universities." *Higher Education in Review* 8: 65–90.

Livingston, Thomas W. 1976. "The Exportation of American Higher Education to West Africa: Liberia College, 1850–1900." *Journal of Negro Education* 45 (3): 246–62. https://doi.org/10.2307/2966902.

Long, B. 2013. "The War on Poverty and Higher Education." Policy Brief 7-13. https://scholar.harvard.edu/files/btl/files/blong_-_war_on_poverty_and _higher_education_-_policy_brief_7-2013.pdf.

Malaney, G. D. 1987. "A Review of Early Decisions in Adams v. Richardson." In *In Pursuit of Equality in Higher Education*, edited by A. S. Pruitt, 17–22. Dix Hills, NY: General Hall.

Morton, Jennifer M. 2021. *Moving Up without Losing Your Way: The Ethical Costs of Upward Mobility*. Princeton, NJ: Princeton University Press.

New England's First Fruits in Respect, First of the Conversion of Some, Conviction of Divers, Preparation of Sundry of the Indians the Progresse of Learning in the Colledge at Cambridge in Massacusets Bay: With Divers Other Special Matters Concerning the Country. 1643. London.

Regents of the University of California v. Allan Bakke. 1978. 438 U.S. 265.

Reiman, Richard. 1993. *The New Deal and American Youth: Ideas and Ideals in a Depression Decade*. Athens: University of Georgia Press.

Rosehan, D. 1967. "Cultural Deprivation and Learning. An Examination for Learning." In *Education for the Disadvantaged*, edited by H. Miller, 38–42. New York: Free Press.

Samuel, Laura J., Darrell J. Gaskin, Antonio J. Trujillo, Sarah L. Szanton, Andrew Samuel, and Eric Slade. 2021. "Race, Ethnicity, Poverty and the Social Determinants of the Coronavirus Divide: U.S. County-Level Disparities and Risk Factors." *BMC Public Health* 21 (1): 1250. https://doi.org/10.1186 /s12889-021-11205-w.

Schrecker, E. 2020, July 22. "The Bad Old Days." *Chronicle of Higher Education*. https://www.chronicle.com/article/the-bad-old-days.

Schwarz, P. J. 1988. *Twice Condemned: Slaves and the Criminal Laws of Virginia, 1705–1865*. Baton Rouge: Louisiana State University Press.

Second Morrill Act. 1890. 7 U.S.C. § 301 et seq.

Shirley. 2018, May 3. "Chinese Students in the United States from 19th Century to 21th Century." https://commons.trincoll.edu/edreform/2018/05/chinese -students-in-the-united-states-from-19th-century-to-21st-century.

Smithsonian American Art Museum. 2014. "Race Relations during Reconstruction." https://americanexperience.si.edu/wp-content/uploads/2014/09/Racial -Relations-during-Reconstruction_.pdf.

Steinberg, Jacques. 1999, September 15. "Idea of Rewarding 'Strivers' Is Opposed by College Board." *New York Times*.

Thelin, J. R., J. R. Edwards, E. Moyen, J. B. Berger, and M. V. Calkins. 2019. "Higher Education in the United States." https://education.stateuniversity .com/pages/2044/Higher-Education-in-United-States.html.

Thompson, Joseph. 2019, November 10. "The GI Bill Should've Been Race Neutral, Politicos Made Sure It Wasn't." https://www.militarytimes.com/military -honor/salute-veterans/2019/11/10/the-gi-bill-shouldve-been-race-neutral -politicos-made-sure-it-wasnt.

"Timeline: 50 Years of Higher Education." 2016, November 16. Chronicle of Higher Education. https://www.chronicle.com/article/timeline-50-years -of-higher-education.

Trow, Martin A. 2005. "Reflections on the Transition from Elite to Mass to Universal Access: Forms and Phases of Higher Education in Modern Societies since WWII." Berkeley, CA: Institute of Governmental Studies. https:// escholarship.org/uc/item/96p3s213.

United States. 1990. *Equal Employment Opportunity Executive Order 11246, as Amended by Executive Order 11375.* Washington, DC: U.S. Dept. of Labor, Employment Standards Administration, Office of Federal Contract Compliance Programs.

United States. 1933. *Monthly Report of the Federal Emergency Relief Administration.* Washington, DC: U.S. Government Printing Office.

U.S. Congress. 1956. *Veterans' Loan Guaranty Program: Hearings before the United States Senate Committee on Labor and Public Welfare, Subcommittee on Veterans Affairs, Eighty-Fourth Congress, Second Session, on June 20, 21, 1956.*

U.S. Department of Education. n.d. "Lists of Postsecondary Institutions Enrolling Populations with Significant Percentages of Undergraduate Minority Students." Accessed May 7, 2021. https://www2.ed.gov/about/offices/list /ocr/edlite-minorityinst.html.

U.S. Department of Education. 2020a. *The Condition of Education 2020.* NCES 2020-144.

U.S. Department of Education. 2020b. *Upward Bound Program.* CFDA 84.047.

Wilder, Craig Steven. 2013. *Ebony & Ivy: Race, Slavery, and the Troubled History of America's Universities.* New York: Bloomsbury Press.

Xiao, Y. 2015, February. "Chinese Immigrants and Heritage Schools in the United States." UCLA National Heritage Language Resource Center. https://nhlrc.ucla.edu/nhlrc/article/150270.

CHAPTER THREE

At-Risk versus At-Promise: The Deficit Model in Student Success

Let's start by trying to conceptualize a university system where the staff and faculty support the individuals who are present without making an attempt to fix and repair their lives. What does this mean exactly? In such a scenario, staff and faculty members would reach students where they are, acknowledging their skills and expertise, and help them achieve their goals rather than make attempts to correct their knowledge and skills. How would this work exactly? Acknowledging students' existing skills and providing students with meaningful opportunities, rather than addressing perceived deficiencies, will allow students to thrive and grow. All students have a wide variety of different kinds of expertise, but sometimes staff and faculty treat knowledge differently depending on where it came from. Once students' skills are acknowledged and students are given opportunities to use and expand those skills in higher education, they will know they can be their full selves and belong at the college. This chapter explores the background and context of how higher education is addressing deficit thinking, introduces the concepts of the deficit model, and examines how deficit thinking appears within the context of academic libraries.

Determining Students' Skills

In order that we might fully examine this issue, it's important to consider the perspectives that have led to the current state of services being provided. Many colleges offer courses to help students obtain remedial skills, though the perceived lack of certain skills may also be an issue of cultural diversity and access to opportunity. Testing is often cultural, and tests are not always an adequate depiction of a student's skill level (Rosales and Walker 2021). While students do need access to gaining additional skills, they sometimes already have the skills and abilities but need to connect their skills and experiences to what is needed at the college level. Looking at students as needing remedial skills, or thinking that students need something in order to succeed, is one example of the deficit model mindset. Let's take a look at the definition of deficit thinking in depth.

Defining the Deficit Model

The deficit model is a set of theories and ideas positing that students need to be fixed in order to succeed. Deficit thinking is a perspective where individuals consider that the students are solely responsible, or solely to blame, should they succeed or not succeed. This model of thinking considers the individual as self-contained and isolated independently from others. Students are expected to pull themselves up by their bootstraps in this model. However, as mentioned earlier, educators can reframe their understanding as practitioners and as scholars to consider the relationships and connections that exist to support students in pursuing their goals.

Shifting away from that model, the authors recommend using the model of at-promise students. Being able to see students as at-promise can flip the concept of who has skills, by insisting that all students are individuals who have strengths to bring to the table. As individuals, students already have many skills and experiences they need to be successful. We call on educators to see students where they are, to adopt a multicultural way of seeing our students, and to acknowledge their abilities. Furthermore, academia must learn to adapt, in order to enact this new vision, by building new services or modifying others in order to accommodate all individuals. In chapter 7, we will share a process that anyone can use to assist at-promise students and support their goals.

Existing Data on Current Students

The first step individuals can take in their workplace is to collect data and learn a lot about the students, who they are, and what they need. Learning the stories of the students—their histories, backgrounds, and experiences–will help all staff and faculty develop an empathic understanding in the individuals who serve these students. Staff and faculty may make many assumptions about who these students are. For example, when it comes to collecting data, the National Center for Education Statistics (NCES) collects data about student success using a historic data definition for student class called FTFT, or first-time full-time students. This has been criticized as not providing an accurate depiction of the student experience. As Gigi Jones wrote in 2017, this is because the FTFT dataset "doesn't consider non-traditional students, including those who are part-time students and transfers. This is an important point because, over the past decade, the number of non-traditional students has outpaced the increase in traditional students, mostly driven by growth in those who have transferred schools."

Though this data definition to measure student success outcomes has changed, datasets now include enrollment and graduation rates of both nontraditional students and also part time students. Despite this, the datasets may not include students enrolled in online programs or students from other demographics. Some efforts are being made to add these groups of students to standard datasets. In this example, these changes were made to become more inclusive. They may not have been directly attributed to a frame of mind regarding the deficit model framework, but the mere act of including more students into the definitions that summarize total student success and outcomes measures is a fantastic example of what we can do when we shift our mindsets.

As staff and faculty learn more about the individuals they admit and serve, it's important to recognize that the students have skills to uncover and prior learning that can be enhanced and grown. Librarians, staff, and faculty can help students by expanding their horizons, by helping the students develop a growth mindset, and by recognizing their strengths and abilities. What is critical is to understand the situational nature of the students and recognize that the individuals experiencing systemic inequity are not to blame for their own inequities.

At-Promise Students

In 2012, researchers at Ferris State University wrote a report about the term "at-risk" and recommended using the term "at-promise" instead. Overall, Fulmer et al. request we make "an institutional shift in redefining students from 'at risk' to 'at promise'" in order to establish "an academic self-concept in which students perceive their strengths." When we work with students to engage with their existing skills to help them to build—authentically—additional skills that will help them succeed, we help students view their own educational career as one that might benefit them rather than one that will assist them in dropping out. Their self-concept may change and allow greater aptitude to achieve their goals.

It can be safe to assume that a common goal among students who choose to enter the university setting are doing so in order to graduate from the university. Beyond the goal of graduation, when they apply to college, become admitted to college, and enter college, they have additional specific goals in mind. They enter college with the desire to have their lives changed, often with the intention of improving their communities. These students, when they enter college, should be provided the opportunity to thrive rather than be questioned for their ability to succeed. Success for all students seems to be socially constructed. The ability to succeed, as others define it, is most certainly socially constructed.

Often universities commend a positive attitude to help individuals achieve their goals. While it may be true that a positive attitude can be helpful, a positive attitude cannot make up for systemic inequities. Only the systems themselves must change in order to stop being as inequitable as they are. University staff and librarians can collaborate to make these changes. Eamon Tewell describes this well in the article "The Problem with Grit: Dismantling Deficit Thinking in Library Instruction" (2020). The concepts of the grit and the growth mindsets have become increasingly popular especially as advice or training for students who are perceived to need additional help. This continues the notion that the students need to be fixed in order that they might succeed.

Fulmer et al. (2012) encouraged educators to shift the perspective in language and understanding on student success from at-risk to at-promise. They point out a number of aspects of this transition that are incredibly valuable to consider. Using the term "at-risk" as a label itself is meaningful enough. Students who are identified this way, who have educational needs below the college level, may experience less success simply because of the term. They state that use of this term, "may undermine the success of these students by implying that they are starting from a deficit point of overcoming obstacles" (Fulmer et al. 2012, p. 1). They recommend restructuring the systems within the university to support these students and create opportunities for them to thrive. They ask to start by deconstructing the "at-risk" label.

By adopting a new phrase, calling in peers and colleagues, and having them consider who they are including while they design or redesign new services, one can start to deconstruct this term. A next step following the adoption of new language is to ensure that the right stakeholders are at the table and are included during evaluation of services. This kind of work can take place on the ground, even if individuals are not in leadership positions. In leadership positions, individuals can deconstruct this label through education, framing, scoping, and stakeholder analysis.

This shift requires educators and leaders in higher education to consider moving forward together with the students. Fulmer et al. (2012) state, "This shift in terminology encourages community colleges to become learning organizations where the belief in students' promise is a shared philosophy" (p. 2). Staff and faculty in higher education can create opportunities for students and lead discussions in their communities and departments in order to initiate a conversation about this shift. Holding dialogues on this topic is crucial for furthering reform and may be the only way to dismantle some of the systemic issues that lead to students who do not succeed. In order to shift that result, higher education does need to change the systems in place to better support those students who are at-promise. It takes change of mind-shift proportions on the part of individuals working within the organization to build in this way.

Statewide Models to Support Students

An example of how to start shifting the conversation would be the Washington [State] Student Achievement Council (WSAC). WSAC is a nine-member council that includes five citizens, among them at least one college student. Students serve on WSAC and work together with leaders to develop greater opportunities for students to succeed. The council's goals include its aim to "improve student success by setting minimum college admission standards and by supporting students' transitions through all phases of education." Its stated vision is, "We inspire and foster excellence in educational attainment." It works with colleges and educators across the state of Washington to improve educational outcomes, especially by focusing on demographics such as race, engaging students and leaders to foster educational attainment for all. It models how students may be able to be supported.

The WSAC annual conference became a regular online webinar for engagement called Pave the Way. GEAR UP, an acronym that stands for Gaining Early Awareness and Readiness for Undergraduate Programs, is one of its programs. Funded federally, GEAR UP works to support low-income students to enable them to enter, succeed in, and graduate from colleges and universities. FuturesNW is one nonprofit program that WSAC highlights. It works with students in high schools to learn about the process of becoming a college student. Ninety-five percent of the students who participate in FuturesNW get into a college of their choice.

Making this shift is important on an institutional and systemic level. But in addition, each individual working in higher education may be able to transition independently. We can each become student-centered practitioners by acknowledging the richness of expertise all of our students have and by seeking to create more opportunities for them. Individually, educators must see all students as individuals with a lot of skills and experiences to offer. What's critical here is for educators to evaluate their own perspectives and challenge them in order to adopt an at-promise mindset.

Flaws in Deficit Thinking

Curt Dudley-Marling is an expert educational researcher and scholar focusing on improving student success outcomes in the school system. In the article "The Resilience of Deficit Thinking" (2015), Dudley-Marling discusses how resistant educators are to critiquing the deficit-thinking model. In many other views, individuals who don't succeed in the school system are blamed for same. In a distributed-self model, one where individuals are defined by how they make connections through relationship and action, it is our responsibility to care for, support, and advocate for students. Dudley-Marling writes, "It takes a community of people doing just the right things in the right time and place for a student to fail in school." In the social-constructivist model, deficit thinking is challenged and would create affordances for all learners, regardless of their background or situation. By accepting deficit thinking, individuals serving those in poverty, for example, would remove blame from the community of educators and advisors serving those students and push it back upon the students in that situation, which to clarify is not what we advocate in this book. Dudley-Marling also criticizes the teacher as a savior model, which also fuels deficit thinking.

An alternative to this perspective is to take an optimistic counternarrative. In this narrative, all of the students are smart and capable. They all come with experiences that enable them to be successful. This shifts the success from students to a dependence on how educators support the students. Dudley-Marling states that this frame would assist educators in seeing ways to expand their knowledge because this narrative "helps lead educators to focus on expanding students' affordances for learning, instead of trying to fix children, their families, or culture."

Consider these concepts with the example of the students who are strivers. One aspect of strivers is that as individual students, they may feel pressure to give up aspects of their life, or parts of their culture or family, in order to succeed in higher education. Dr. Jennifer Morton's work challenges this notion. In her book *Moving Up Without Losing Your Way: The Ethical Costs of Upward Mobility* (2019), Dr. Morton poses a reframe for students and learners who sought to improve their life without losing their background. How might we work to support learners so that they do not need to give up their family, culture, or life? We might consider ways to expand their knowledge and to provide pathways to what they would like to accomplish while helping them support their families.

Dudley-Marling explains that educators can support these students by creating high expectations in coursework, confronting the deficit narrative, and looking for ways to enhance students' pathways to their goals. Students are not deficient except in a lack of opportunities for thoughtful, engaging learning (2015. Librarians in academic libraries can assist in many ways, including but not limited to (1) creating services that meet students 24/7 and that can be accessed by all students regardless of technology or location and (2) creating multicultural instructional platforms.

Eamon Tewell and John Agada are two library and information science scholars who have addressed the issue of deficit thinking within the context of academic libraries. Tewell addresses the concepts of the grit-and-growth mindset, while Agada addresses the concept of students that are at-risk. Both have worked to address how librarians are poised to dismantle these notions and become student success–driven educators. These authors' works are important, and we can build on their ideas. With their texts as foundations, we can work to involve multicultural curriculum design and adopt an equity lens in library instruction and service design.

Agada is critical of the idea that students are at-risk and how that becomes interpreted in academic libraries. In his article "Deconstructing the At-Risk Student Phenomenon: Can Librarian Values Salvage Education for the 21st Century?" Agada illustrates how traditional library instruction has focused on perceived deficiencies in learners even though libraries have values of equity and diversity (2001, p. 81). He posits that academic libraries may be able to lead within the education system by using these values in support of students. Students from a wide variety of backgrounds and experiences enter the school system. As described in the previous chapter, students labeled "strivers" are forced to make a choice between their family or culture and being able to achieve in the education system. Agada describes this in terms of cultural capital: "The school learning environment affirms and rewards those who exhibit the dominant cultural capital, which the teacher often exhibits by virtue of her race, ethnicity, or class" (2001, p. 82). Tewell discusses the role a librarian or educator can play in this by encouraging educators to share more about themselves with students: "Instructors might share their own background and context, modeling a degree of vulnerability before asking students to share" (2020, p. 152). What is important here as a key takeaway is that teachers reveal something about themselves—for example, if they are first in their family to attend college—or discuss how they first became familiar with some of the concepts they are discussing. This creates pathways between the student and the teacher and allows the students to see additional opportunities.

What Agada describes is that those who are not adept at navigating the cultural aspects of the education system will be labeled "at-risk" of failing in school. This label perpetuates negative connotations and isolates the students who come from underrepresented cultures. When they share their experiences, they are dismissed. Agada writes that this dismissal is "reflective of the nature of scholarship and knowledge legitimized by the school system" (2001, p. 83). The words we use to substantiate student speech and culture are critically important to their success. As educators, librarians can support, acknowledge, and empower voices.

Agada describes the mechanisms by which minority students are displaced within the classroom setting due to the lack of perceived value of their cultural experiences. He states that this directly relates to lowered expectations for such students. When this occurs, students perform less. When we apply higher expectations to our work, all students perform at the highest levels. High-impact practices are a key component to helping students succeed. Agada points to how this has been problematic in academic libraries.

He states that the neutrality of libraries overpowers the value of social responsibility (2001, p. 84). Academic librarians must uphold the important values of social responsibility and equity and serve the individual students at our institutions. Agada states, "A window of opportunity exists for academic libraries today to practice what they preach, thereby leading their parent institutions by example" (2001). However, merely presenting access to information will not be sufficient in creating equal opportunities for all students.

Librarian Responsibilities

To some degree, as educators, we do have a responsibility to advocate for our students. There is a large disparity with regard to educational success among a variety of demographic factors that need to be taken into account. How are we able to confront this without deconstructing our systems and approaches? By becoming an at-promise educator or an at-promise institution, we would be able to recognize the multiple perspectives and expertise that each student brings to the landscape and be able to contextualize learning through that individualistic and pluralistic lens. When we do so, we empower students to focus on their growth and skills.

Tewell suggests that deficit thinking is furthered through our library instruction programs and ought to be modified with intervention. Agada agrees, and both argue for specific interventions that libraries can put into place. By using specific practices and collaborating with others across the college campus, librarians are in a unique position to use their value system in order to better support the at-promise student.

Let's explore some of these practices here, though many of them will be described at a deeper level in chapter 6, where we explore the history of student success in academic libraries. Agada calls for learning about the individuals who are identified as at-risk students at their institutions. By learning about these students, librarians can better understand their specific contexts. Furthermore, library instruction can incorporate a wide variety of cultural dispositions instead of starting from a single dominant cultural paradigm. Tewell agrees that librarians can do this and can share something about their experiences with their students in order to walk with students from their experiences into a place of shared expertise.

Both Agada and Tewell advocate for the use of critical pedagogy in the library instruction program. Agada shares that critical pedagogy assumes "all knowledge is socially constructed, seeks to empower all students, not only at-risk students, to engage in cultural criticism by appropriating knowledge outside their own experience, so as to broaden their understanding of themselves, their worlds, and the possibilities for transforming the assumptions about their conditions" (2001, p. 85). This would allow students to use information frameworks to think about how to solve problems within their communities. Another way to address this is by using the design-thinking frameworks. This framework is expanded upon in part 3 of this book and includes a step in design to develop empathy for the individuals you are designing for. This may also be of use in this context as they begin with developing empathy for the students you are teaching. Academic librarians who have instruction responsibilities can teach design thinking and also use it in instruction by learning as much as possible about the users you are designing for and then helping construct new knowledge accordingly.

On Belonging

In the seminal text "Marginality and Mattering: Key Issues in Building Community" (1989), the author, Nancy Schlossberg, discusses concepts to wholly involve all students in the process of learning and creating new knowledge. Some of the key aspects of this core work on student success include the idea that a focus on what connects us is critical to supporting our students. Schlossberg describes the ways in which individuals can move back and forth from being considered marginal to feeling as though they matter. Though everyone—and every student—will feel marginal occasionally, it takes a concerted effort to help facilitate mattering on a college campus.

Through connection, individuals may be able to make others feel that they matter and believe that they are important. Institutions may be able to facilitate this process by creating rituals, celebrating successes, and creating environments designed to support all students. Schlossberg explains that this will lead students to become more involved in the college environment: "The creation of environments that clearly indicate to all students that they matter will urge them to greater involvement" (1989). By working together with individuals across campus on how to make an at-promise learning environment, we can help students realize how much they do matter to us. This can be both on an individual level and an institutional and strategic level. We can communicate the concept of "mattering" to students, letting them know they belong and they matter to staff and faculty, by confronting services that only function in a deficit model and instead creating services that switch to an at-promise structure.

Equity Gaps and Collaborations

Hrabowski, Henderson, and Tracy (2020) report that 60 percent of all students who enroll in higher education graduate but that only 40 percent of Black students who enroll in higher education graduate. Furthermore, they conclude, "It would be simplistic—and wrong—to conclude that our students of color are failing. Instead, we must admit that higher education is failing them." What we need is not to approach our students to fix them but instead to fix the systems and institutions that are failing them. By working with stakeholders, learning from students, and creating support mechanisms for those students, staff and faculty can combat ineffectual systems.

Ultimately, the researchers at Ferris State University call for the use of collaborations in higher education institutions. Fulmer et al. state that making these "formalized networks will allow institutions to develop a set of guiding principles, and then apply these to all forms of educational approaches to help build a harmonious learning environment" (2012, p. 3). We reiterate that creating cross-unit connections will help establish networks to support students. As we create new services and new approaches to services and we develop a new understanding about our students, we will evolve the pathways within the institution to become more supportive: to assist us in our mission to help all students succeed and to create an at-promise institution of learning.

There are other aspects that we can take away from some of this work. For one, at the core of this work is the understanding that we must advocate for our students. We also must offer them opportunities for success. As we develop our services, we must add cultural touchpoints within our instruction and learning environments in whatever ways we can. Environments must offer signs of reflection—that is, for students to see their own culture reflected in the learning environment. As librarians, advisors, staff, and faculty in higher education, we ought to be responsible for our part in our students' success.

Recommendations for Instructional Practices

Agada points out many practices that librarians can adopt to bridge the gaps. These practices can also be adopted by anyone else in higher education who wants to make an impact in students' lives. Changing one's own mindset to see what students have to offer rather than what they do not is one significant starting point. Librarians can develop a path of self-reflection and begin to learn more, through this book as one example, about what an at-promise student can offer. Avoiding using terms such as "at-risk" or "marginalized" to describe a population matters, too, because how we refer to others impacts how we think about them, and what we think can impact our actions.

Hiring a diverse set of librarians to work in a library is important. Ensure that hires come from a diverse set of backgrounds, including socioeconomic. This will help avoid having a monoculture and a groupthink mindset but will also provide librarians who have similar social or cultural touchpoints to the students they serve. Faculty who have had similar experiences to the students can create many pathways to success simply by being present and acknowledging the similarities. Agada describes a child arriving at school with a toolbox with which to learn: the toolbox comes with tools learned in social, cultural, and economic circumstances. The cultural capital may not be valued at the institution, which can impede the learner's ability to succeed in that context. Agada (2001, p. 83) points out that "the academic performance of at-risk students may therefore represent less of their individual competence, and more of the school's depreciation of their cultural capital." A solution to this is to have a diverse group of librarians who can see the value of the toolboxes each learner brings and to have librarians trained to see those tools as well.

Providing for a stronger multicultural framework within an academic library is a substantial goal. Agada states that the cultural dissonance learners experience between their lives and the college landscape can narrowed through education: "Academic librarians ought to educate themselves about at-risk students and their communities, and support research and documentation of knowledge about them. They should also advocate infusion of critical information literacy skills and culturally diverse content in all academic curricula and library resources. Secondly, as academic librarians engage in their instructional roles, they must provide opportunities to connect with every student in the class by using curricula content and teaching methods that draw on students' cultural backgrounds, experiences, interests and learning styles, irrespective of subject matter being taught."

Agada (2001) makes several points here:

- Librarians need to learn about the at-promise students they serve.
- Librarians can collect and document what they learn about those communities.
- Librarians should have culturally diverse content in all of their instruction programs.
- Librarians ought to connect to every student.

Using critical pedagogy, which articulates that all knowledge is created culturally, should also go a long way in helping facilitate student success. Students' prior experiences and conversations can help connect them to their current experiences in college. This can set a pathway of achievement.

Agada also points out that setting high expectations can help. This can be accomplished by creating solid opportunities. For example, as will be explained throughout chapter 8, which addresses the role of emerging technologies in student success, makerspaces offer complex opportunity networks. Students can enter into a makerspace regardless of where they are coming from and set about a tangible course of inquiry making and creating research ideas.

Now that you've learned a lot of the theoretical background, let's put these ideas into a practical set of recommendations you can use.

Preparation for the Work

Librarians ought to be engaging in a continual process of self-development, honest self-reflection, and professional development. The purpose in doing so is to reveal biases and habits that preclude practices that may hinder the growth of certain students. Acknowledging bias, and that we all have bias, is the first step in overcoming this possible hindrance. Even in *Spider-Man: Into the Spider-Verse*, Spiderman states that step 3 in his plans is to reexamine his personal biases; we share this detail to reinforce how the practice has seeped into the current culture.

There are many ways to go about dealing with personal biases, but here are the processes we advocate for individuals to adopt:

1. As an individual, participate in independent learning opportunities such as personal bias training and tests.

    In all cases, it is entirely up to individuals to share what they would like, if anything at all, with others. There should be no expectation in a workplace to take an internal bias test and share those results with coworkers. If individuals do participate in such a thing as a group, they can share their thoughts on the overall experience, but no one should require an individual to share the results. These results should be used in order to grow as individuals.

    There are many tests, but we recommend two: the Harvard Implicit Bias Association Tests and the Kirwan Institute Implicit Bias Training (Implicit Bias Module Series n.d.). Participating in these independently can help you reflect on your own feelings and attitudes. We recommend that you take these tests and modules over time and evaluate how you feel about other individuals. Your biases may change how you approach working with others.

2. Participate in group trainings on diversity, equity, inclusion, and belonging.

    Many organizations offer this kind of training. If you work at a college or university, you may be able to take part in training offered. It's important to participate in these in order to learn more, especially about populations with whom you are least familiar.

3. Join a group or intergroup dialogue.

    Intergroup dialogues are private and personal spaces where individuals can share their thoughts and feelings together in order to process them. Sometimes this offers a way to reflect as a group and reimagine other ways to react and respond in any social activity, including workplaces.

4. Consider communication styles.

    Individuals from different places and backgrounds use different styles of communication. Though a student may not be using a type of communication you are familiar with or accustomed to using, that may not mean the student must conform to your personal standards of communication. Each culture has different styles with specific communication traits, such as linear or circular, direct or indirect, assertive or passive, among others (La Brack 2003). Becoming more aware of those styles and that anyone may use any type at any time is important in working with students.

5. Adopt open communication styles.

    A good model for communication can be the Open the Front Door communication model. This model provides steps to use to share observations with others and express what they wish could be different (Souza 2015). Practicing being accountable to your own thoughts and feelings by sharing them with others in the workplace can really change the way you approach your work. In addition, it's important to practice receiving feedback and hearing what others wish as well.

6. Intentionally create a healthy work culture.

    As a manager or supervisor, it can be easier to set and establish a workplace culture, but everyone has a role to play in creating a healthy work environment. Not spreading gossip, not speaking ill of students, and holding yourself and others accountable are all ways to set a healthy workplace culture. There are many trainings and practices that workplaces can adopt, including those available from databases and resources such as Franklin Covey or LinkedIn Learning. A workplace striving to become a healthy work environment would also have a goal about the culture in the strategic plan.

Library Instruction Recommendations

Now let's look at how we can approach students from a multicultural perspective that encourages belonging and allows students to form deeper learning connections.

1. Gain attention.

    When librarians are designing instruction and outreach, they have a variety of instructional models to use, such as ARCS (Attention, Relevance, Competence, Satisfaction) and ADDIE (Analyze, Develop, Design, Implement, Evaluate), which can be used together to create library instruction (Kurt 2018). The ARCS model ("ARCS Model of Motivation" n.d.) presents "Attention" as the first key step in delivering instruction. The ADDIE model asks instructors to consider "Analysis" as the first step. The Analysis phase in ADDIE is where one considers the audience and identifies the goals for the instruction. The Attention phase in ARCS refers to making connections with the students. Both steps are key to reaching students where they are. Learn as much as possible about the students both before the course and continually throughout the instruction. Use examples that truly gain their attention and are current and relevant to their experiences. Their local community and campus are great resources to start with when introducing material.

2. Identify attributes to share.

    Our respective identities contain many different aspects. Share what you are comfortable with, and students may find more comfort and belonging. Examples of this may include, as applicable, talking about your low-income upbringing, being a striver and defining what a striver is, being queer and what that means, your ethnicity or background, places where you have lived or grown up, whether you have disabilities, and so forth. Whatever you are willing to share will help groups of students feel more at ease in the instruction.

    Making these kinds of social connections is important in asynchronous and synchronous learning modes. In the online classroom this is as important, if not more so, as helping students find social engagement and connection. Be intentional about what you choose to share and ensure you do not require students to share information about themselves.

3. Evaluate examples.

    What kinds of examples are you using in your instruction or outreach? Be extremely mindful to use examples that are diverse and on which you are knowledgeable. Diversity can take many forms, including income diversity. One common example is to show practical databases, such as MEDLINE, which shares authoritative medical information, when introducing databases to students. Examples of what to search should also be diverse and come from a wide variety of places.

Partnership Types

Through partnerships, especially with students and student groups, libraries can employ a form of participatory librarianship. Participatory librarianship is a type of action research where the researcher partners with the individuals they serve to create new services. For example, a librarian could partner with teens who use the library to redesign the teen section of the library. Partnering with users to redesign services should result in positive changes for the users being served. In the health profession, this is referred to as "collaborative-based participatory research." Students who want to bring about events or lectures can seek support for their initiative from the library. This can be through any aspect of the library, regardless of the unit. This helps the library educate the campus community and provide alternative viewpoints, as Agada points out (2001, p. 86): "By building such activities around at-risk students, their faculty, and peers, the library would be providing opportunities to broaden perspectives, and hopefully reduce social isolation and stigma for at-risk students." In any case, hiring students to review the work of the library, and also to work to serve the library, can help. By partnering with students as employees, library staff can create a better set of services within the library.

Data Collection

In all services on a college campus, it can be important to focus on who is using the services. This can ensure that all practices taking place are inclusive of all. Once individuals are on campus, their demographic facts and figures should be published. These are generally available digitally and published on a university or college website.

Any service should correspond in terms of demographic breakdown to what is represented on the college campus. The breakdown of users of a specific service that is voluntary to participate in should mimic the same demographic breakdown as is on a campus. For example, if a college campus is 51 percent women, the service perhaps ought to serve the same percentage of women. If those breakdowns are not the same—if for some reason they are higher or lower—it may be something to look into, depending on the results and after some analysis and conversation. In many cases, "data dashboards," websites that depict summaries of data, such as grades by student demographic, can be time-consuming to create. Nevertheless, staff and faculty ought to actively recruit to underrepresented groups if that is not occurring naturally, not only to recruit students to the specific programs staff might work for but to the college or university itself as well.

In the next chapter, we will take a look at how libraries have historically attempted to meet the needs of a diverse population. In addition, we will look into how academic libraries have made efforts to eliminate a deficit-thinking mindset in their work. Services, programs, and educational strategies are all kinds of efforts academic libraries have undertaken to make this change. How might academic libraries best meet this need, learn from what has come before, and work to the future?

References

Agada, John. 2001. "Deconstructing the At-Risk Student Phenomenon: Can Librarian Values Salvage Education for the 21st Century?" ACRL Tenth National Conference, 81–88.

"ARCS Model of Motivation." n.d. Texas Tech University. Accessed March 22, 2022. http://www.tamus.edu/academic/wp-content/uploads/sites/24/2017/07 /ARCS-Handout-v1.0.pdf.

Dudley-Marling, Curt. 2015. "The Resilience of Deficit Thinking." *Journal of Teaching and Learning* 10 (1). https://jtl.uwindsor.ca/index.php/jtl/article /view/4171/pdf.

Fulmer, Mara Jevera, David Wildfong, Matthew Chaney, Adam L. Cloutier, Deborah Coates, Alexandria Densmore, Lesley Frederick, et al. 2012. "Moving from At Risk to At Promise: A Paradigm Shift for Community Colleges Addressing Underprepared Students." *At Issue* 2 (1): 1–6.

Hrabowski, Freeman A., III, Peter H. Henderson, and J. Kathleen Tracy. 2020. "Higher Education Should Lead the Efforts to Reverse Structural Racism." *The Atlantic.* https://www.theatlantic.com/ideas/archive/2020/10 /higher-education-structural-racism/616754.

"Implicit Bias Module Series." n.d. Kirwan Institute for the Study of Race and Ethnicity. Accessed March 22, 2022. http://kirwaninstitute.osu.edu/implicit -bias-training.

Jones, Gigi. 2017. "Expanding Student Success Rates to Reflect Today's College Students." *NCES Blog.* https://nces.ed.gov/blogs/nces/post/expanding -student-success-rates-to-reflect-today-s-college-students.

Kurt, Serhat. 2018. "ADDIE Model Instructional Design." Educational Technology. https://educationaltechnology.net/the-addie-model-instructional-design.

La Brack, Bruce. 2003. "What's Up with Culture?" https://www2.pacific.edu/sis /culture.

Morton, J. M. 2019. *Moving up without losing your way.* Princeton, NJ: Princeton University Press.

Rosales, John, and Tim Walker. 2021, March 20. "The Racist Beginnings of Standardized Testing." NEA News. https://www.nea.org/advocating-for-change /new-from-nea/racist-beginnings-standardized-testing.

Schlossberg, Nancy K. 1989. "Marginality and Mattering: Key Issues in Building Community." *New Directions for Student Services* 48 (1): 5–15.

Souza, Tasha. 2015. "Open the Front Door Communication Framework." https:// www.csun.edu/sites/default/files/OpenTheFrontDoor.pdf.

Tewell, Eamon. 2020. "The Problem with Grit: Dismantling Deficit Thinking in Library Instruction." *Portal: Libraries and the Academy* 20 (1): 137–59.

CHAPTER FOUR

Boise State University: A Case Study

Boise State University is a doctorate-granting, public university located in Boise, Idaho, that started from humble beginnings. Though Boise State has reached the level of a Tier 2 Carnegie Classification of Higher Education, it was founded as a community college in 1932. In less than 100 years, Boise State rose from a community college to its current status, and as a result, its unique culture involves rural partnerships, online learning, and a large commuting student population. This rise can be attributed to the innovative practices taking place at the university and also the unique aspects of the location and greater context.

Located in southwestern Idaho, the identity of the area is shared between the Pacific Northwest and the Mountain West. The state contains midsize urban and rural communities spread across the vast state. As a result of the large geography of the area, regions relate to the neighboring communities along the border closest to them. These areas include Oregon, Washington, Utah, Montana, Wyoming, and the Canadian province of British Columbia. Boise itself is incredibly isolated from other major metropolitan areas. Salt Lake City is a four-hour drive southeast. Mountains, ranches, farms, and small towns fill the landscape. The second major metropolitan area close to Boise is Portland, Oregon. A more than six-hour drive from Boise, Portland differs from Boise with respect to demographics, politics, geography, and economics. Boise is a midsize urban area with about 260,000 residents in the city and 462,000 residents in the greater metropolitan area. As a result, Boise retains a small-town feel though it is one of the fastest-growing cities in the country, often identified as growing at an unsustainable rate and creating conflict for all residents, including students, due to a lack of housing availability and income stagnation.

These factors make southwestern Idaho a distinct region in which students have unique needs. Though Idaho is a predominantly rural state geographically, the demographics of the state have a skewed population, with the majority living in the Boise metro area. What comes out of this dichotomy is a confluence of ideas from both rural and urban areas. This creates very important discourse, where diverse ideas and unique solutions can take hold. Students from rural areas can participate in action research through Boise State University that seeks to benefit their communities. All the while, Boise State continues to help support students from this wide variety of backgrounds to help them graduate.

The university produces graduates from a wide variety of doctoral and master's degree programs, certifications, and more. Due to high research activity, Boise State University advanced to its Tier 2 classification. Like all other universities and colleges during the COVID pandemic, the faculty and staff pivoted their teaching and research to adapt to operate under suboptimal conditions. Adapting to meet needs throughout the pandemic has been an ongoing challenge for all universities. However, there are several ways in which Boise State customized support to meet the changing needs of students, who faced challenges at this time, and staff and faculty helped pivot programs to remote learning.

Supporting faculty members during the pandemic is a great example of the unique and innovative culture at Boise State. In this way, the university came up with support structures tailored to the individual in a way that helps support the university. Faculty pivoted their courses to emergency remote, though some others took the time to invest in creating high-enrollment and high-impact online courses.

Through a program initiated through the provost's office, called a Faculty Evaluation Procedural Appendix, faculty are allowed to account for their individual experience during the pandemic. This appendix, like any program designed for success, acknowledges differences in individual needs. This program allowed faculty to make adjustments to account for the shifts in teaching and research. By creating this new program, faculty could have some agency over their workload and could choose to make an adjustment. For example, were faculty members impacted by taking care of parents or children during the pandemic, they could select teaching, service, or scholarship as a place to reduce workload from a certain percentage to lower. That meant that if you previously had a zero-percentage workload in an area, if you did any work in that area, it would be considered exceeding expectations. There was no system in place to declare reasons for opting in—just the simple acknowledgment that all individuals experienced the pandemic differently. For some, the conditions became more favorable, whereas for others they were less so. Some increased their caretaker responsibilities to family members, significantly, and some became ill from COVID.

The ability to connect multiple systems and show care to students, staff, and faculty is an integral part of the culture at Boise State. The key themes are innovation, strengths mindset in culling limited resources, and caring for others. Simplified, on campus this is called "blue turf thinking" as a nod to the uniquely blue football field that the Boise State Broncos play on. While it is hard to say that the program for faculty during COVID will result in long-term change or success among faculty, it certainly shows how nimble the organization can be to make adjustments intended to benefit all. By having a willingness to change systems, we can focus so much more on how to best meet the needs of those before us. As staff and faculty are the architects of these systems, staff and faculty can change and manage the systems in a way that benefits students.

Pandemic cultural shifts on campus included changes in policy affecting students. Students were also able to make a choice about their grades. They have many programs that served their success during the pandemic, but in addition, they were able to review their letter grades and, if they preferred, to switch to a pass/not-pass option for their final grade. Students, in light of the impact of the pandemic on their ability to sustain previous academic success, could protect their overall GPA—for example, by changing a C on a transcript to a P (Passing).

Demographic Considerations

Prior to the pandemic, the university demonstrated a strong focus on student success, developing programs for many different kinds of students to support their academic path. For example, Boise State hosts a large population of students returning after absence due to academic dismissal, changes in home life, or a desire to join the workforce. The campus offers programs and support systems to returning students. Students who may drop out due to grades, for example, take courses and receive academic rehabilitation when they return. Rehabilitation may involve enrollment in academic success courses, in which instructors provide opportunities for students to learn about how the university system works, build social capital, increase academic skills, focus on their goals, and learn about university resources.

The authors of this book taught an academic success course, Academic 102: Academic Recovery and Success. (The course designation "Academic" encompasses a series of courses designed to provide opportunities for students to gain success skills at the university. Academic 106 was also a previously offered course: the library skills and information literacy course.) For Academic 102 (also called ACAD102), many of the students who enroll fall into several of the at-promise groups listed in previous chapters. This course focuses on study skills, learning about the resources on campus, acquiring knowledge about one's own strengths, and receiving tips on how to improve schoolwork. This class often has high enrollment, as it is a requirement for students who are in academic recovery and reentering the university. It has benefited many students who have taken it. As the data ecosystem at Boise State is still developing, data are not available to track those students and their graduation rates. There is anecdotal evidence in that students have written to the faculty instructors to share stories about how the course benefited them and let the instructors know that they were graduating.

The students enrolling in this course may do so for a number of reasons. They may want to boost their GPA or gain study skills that will benefit them. They may be returning to school after a time away. Some have caretaking responsibilities. Many have full-time jobs and take care of their family. Aside from the anecdotes of experiences with the students in this class, it's important to consider the demographics. As a call to action, it would be useful for anyone using this book to design additional services to acquire a demographic listing of their home institution. Chapter 8 discusses the role of makerspaces, emerging technologies, and design thinking in creating support for these students. The course design of Academic 102 included lesson plans, modules, and experiences using these tools, so chapter 8 also includes some of those lesson plans, to be used and replicated in other institutions.

Boise State University has a student body with a large number of students who are caregivers. Boise State seniors spend, on average, more than 9 hours per week caring for dependents. According to National Survey of Student Engagement (NSSE) data collected in 2015, as explained by Nick Warcholak (2021) at Boise State University, Boise State students do more caregiving each week than students at peer institutions: "First-year Boise State students spend about the same amount of time caring for dependents as students at peer institutions, 3.9 hours a week. Our seniors, however, spend significantly more time caring for dependents than students at peer institutions, 9.4 hours to 6.3 hours per week." In 2018, this number appeared to drop, however, and seniors in 2018 at Boise State reported only about 6 hours per week. Boise State has been admitting increasing numbers of traditional students, and so the drop could be correlated to this factor.

But it still represents around three hours more per week than for students of 24 other identified peer institutions in a recent report. The students in this group are taking care of family members, and it's important to understand what that represents. Some have children and families of their own. Others are caring for a sick relative. Some have parents with illnesses who are on hospice care. Their family obligations require a substantial amount of time and energy.

Mental health concerns are another reason Boise State students drop out, and the campus faces unique needs to meet these concerns. The overarching culture of Idaho draws heavily from libertarian ideals and rugged individualism in which students often feel and believe that mental health support is not for them, that they must persist in taking care of themselves. Some students on campus face a cultural stigma with regard to accessing mental health resources. Students enter crisis, and there are often not enough services for their needs. One opportunity to grow is to increase campus-wide knowledge regarding how to recognize trauma. In addition, staff and faculty can also redesign services to become trauma informed. Academic 102 developed trauma-informed practices to care for those students, and the campus makerspace also adopted trauma-informed approaches to students. This is an important idea to consider, especially after the global pandemic and societal upheaval. Many students have been impacted by the historic events taking place recently and as a result have experienced trauma and loss.

Meanwhile Boise State has increasing enrollments of overall students but especially "nontraditional," students who are characterized by some combination of veteran status, age over 25, returning after a change in career or in parenting or caregiving responsibilities, and returning after incarceration. The incoming class for the 2019–2020 year was 34 percent first-generation college students (Boise State University 2019), and overall, the entire student population contained 44 percent first-generation students (Wellness with BroncoFit n.d.). The four-year graduation rate for first-time freshmen who entered in fall 2016 was 38 percent, up from 31 percent the previous year. This rate has increased, which may be attributed to factors that include the admission of traditional students with a stronger support network and a reduction in the number of commuter students. Though procrastination had been previously reported to be the number one barrier facing students at Boise State, according to a survey, their finances and career fall second and third in line (Wellness with BroncoFit n.d.). Forty percent of the students surveyed indicated they were lonely, and 50 percent reported experiencing moderate stress (Wellness with BroncoFit n.d.). In the same survey data, 30 percent reported anxiety.

Students are navigating many of these challenges but sometimes without guidance, support, or connection. This may result in having crucial conversations with students, as they come from such a wide variety of backgrounds and beliefs. Students who arrive at the college or university need guidance and expertise. They sometimes feel vulnerable due to events that take place and need staff and faculty to acknowledge events. In short, as much as staff and faculty need to be heard by students, the opposite is also true. Students need staff to be responsive through listening and recognizing the resources available. It's important to realize that colleges and universities don't have all of the services needed to help students succeed.

Innovation as Culture

In a culture of innovation, trying new things is an important value that is supported by the Boise State. There is a high threshold for trying new tactics and assessing them to determine if they have succeeded or need improvement and if so, how. An organization with silo thinking represents an absence of connection and reflects a culture that does not come together and has no opportunities to connect. Boise State is making those connections and then working together. Everyone can innovate at Boise State, and everyone does. As referenced earlier, on campus this is called blue turf thinking: the idea of seeing a better, faster, and more efficient way to do something unique that best serves the students and community. Even if an organization is somewhere between being siloed and being open and connected, there are ways to find connection and build ideas. For example, when attending large meetings, library employees can work to find like-minded individuals. Using this networking strategy, you can meet with other folks who do not necessarily work with you regularly but who have similar goals. If a college or university hosts quarterly and annual meetings, it's important to sit with new or unfamiliar groups to get to know them and create that space for connection. By making a plan to have deliberate attendance at interdisciplinary meetings, such as pedagogical workshops, learning opportunities, or lectures, one can meet many more individuals to find common ground. Looking for that commonality and having conversations can set the stage to build new opportunities.

Another aspect of Boise State innovative culture is that folks will often refer to others in their own network. A common happenstance is that in talking about one's own interests, someone will recommend others with similar interests to meet with. While there is no official method for doing this, harnessing passions and making networked connections are a practice embedded in the culture of the institution. As a result, if staff or faculty members advocate for a change, they can often pursue those ideas so long as they fit the mission and goals of the units and institution.

Practical Insights from the Albertsons Library MakerLab

The MakerLab at Albertsons Library offers services for students to gain access, coaching, and instruction in the use of emerging technologies and tools. They can make projects of their own choosing or to meet the needs of an academic assignment. They find a community of other learners in the space. They often discuss the identities and challenges they face, as well as commonalities, while they engage in the making process.

The level of engagement in a makerspace is high. In some courses or on a campus, students may disengage. Within a makerspace, through ongoing conversation, that disengagement is sometimes due to the students wanting to make a big difference, to make a substantial change in the world around them, to improve the lives of individuals in their communities. They may need tangible, practical, experiential learning techniques to help them connect to content.

The employees who coach and teach in the Albertsons Library MakerLab acknowledge that everyone is a maker and everyone is an expert. Expertise is not always obvious or visible, but it is present. Often, students may not know what they are experts in. Everyone can learn from others, and that's especially true in a makerspace. Users can teach staff and faculty new information just as much as the other way around. Library workers can use microempowerments to elevate students by acknowledging what they have done or created. "Microempowerment" is a term used at the Boise State MakerLab to describe a way to share with individuals who you see are learning or have learned something new or who are showing their expertise in an area. One example would be to share with a student that the student explained something very well to someone else. Another example could be technical, such as sharing how much the student has learned about the settings on a 3D printer. This is especially helpful as a reframing for students when they may express frustration about something, such as when they hit a barrier. A positive culture is one that points out the great things others do in the makerspace.

In the Boise State MakerLab, differences among the users are exactly what helps individuals thrive. The MakerLab and makerspaces in general create space for folks to connect and have healthy kinds of conversations, which can include disagreements. In this process, individuals discuss aspects of their identity and background, sharing experiences and skills, while also setting limits on what is unhealthy and setting boundaries for those appropriately. In makerspaces, these conversations come to the surface quickly because making and identity are intimately tied. Makerspaces, because of that, ought to have employees who can coach others to identify themselves as makers. Some of these techniques include confronting the idea that some individuals don't consider themselves to be good with technology. Employees can ask makers to talk about what they most recently made and break down the steps to show that it is all a matter of following steps to get to a finished prototype.

Beyond the MakerLab at Albertsons Library

Part of the culture at Boise State is to acknowledge that mistakes are a part of the learning process. In the process of making, creating with emerging technologies and other tools, this is particularly true. Telling those stories and connecting with those who want to create are key aspects of the culture and a part of what helps students succeed. Beyond the MakerLab, librarians are partnering with individuals in other campus areas to make improvements for students. These include partnerships with students who are parents. As a result of their high caregiving responsibilities, the library has created family-supportive study rooms and environments that support literacy among children and also help students complete their schoolwork. The Library's STEM toy backpack program was a prototype in this program. The program was an attempt to welcome parent-students into the library and provide fun, educational toys to occupy young children temporarily so the parent-students could focus on their studies. The backpacks would be checked out at the circulation desk. Inside were books and educational toys. The toys included clear plastic magnetic tiles and similar items.

Another example includes research and data visualization partnerships. Recognizing the need for students to develop their expertise in research skills, librarians have partnered with other research staff and faculty to increase their skills and offer workshops for undergraduate researchers. These workshops are popular in part because of the number of undergraduate research presentation opportunities and also because working with faculty on research at Boise State is a very in-demand activity.

References

Boise State University. 2019, November 4. "Boise State Celebrates First Generation College Students." *Boise State News*. https://www.boisestate.edu/news/2019/11/04/boise-state-celebrates-first-generation-college-students.

Warcholak, Nick. 2021. "What Does NSSE Tell Us About How Much Time Boise State Students Spend on Work and Other Responsibilities?" Boise State University. https://d25vtythmttl3o.cloudfront.net/uploads/sites/501/2021/10/What-Does-NSSE-Tell-Us-About-How-Our-Students-Spend-Time-rev-Oct-2021-PDF.pdf.

Wellness with BroncoFit. n.d. "Wellness Facts and Figures." Boise State University. Accessed February 27, 2022. https://www.boisestate.edu/broncofit/wellness-facts-and-figures.

PART 2

Advocacy and Partnerships

CHAPTER FIVE

Student Success Administrators

College and University Units

Universities generally have an academic-focused administrative and teaching unit and a student-focused administrative side. These two divisions should act together to provide for the student experience while guaranteeing a high-quality education. These two separate divisions also have different budget models. In some cases, this reinforces the so-called silo thinking practice, where individuals focus on the exclusive goals of their particular unit without considering the interconnectivity of goals across units. This kind of thinking can contribute to not generating strategies to meet students' needs. This chapter will explore who the student success administrators are and the background of the problems with these kinds of divisions, all in an effort to elucidate ways to collaborate with those individuals, including an interdisciplinary framework to approach solutions.

Within the college or university setting, provosts typically oversee academic areas, and deans or vice presidents lead student affairs–reporting lines. Libraries usually fall on an academic affairs side but sometimes are also included in the student affairs side of an organizational chart, depending on the campus. Libraries therefore can report to a vice president of student affairs or to a dean of students. Advisors are often in student affairs or directly embedded in colleges. Academic librarians are often liaisons to specific disciplines or academic departments. The librarians or library faculty may have advanced degrees and background in those areas, such as a second master's or PhD in addition to an American Library Association–accredited library science master's degree. At other times they can be generalists working with a specific user group. In many academic libraries, librarians are also redefining what it means to be a liaison, what those core responsibilities are, and whom the librarians serve. This chapter presents the possibilities for a student success administrator liaison model so that librarians can begin to work with them in whatever capacity they choose.

Collaborating with administrators or staff whose roles are dedicated to student success within functional areas is a key to unlocking the relevance of the library to our undergraduate students. Partnering across reporting lines and functional areas to deliver new services begins with librarians discovering the professional and campus contexts of student success administrators to create more effective and relevant proposals for partnerships.

Two professional organizations exist to promote professional development, scholarship, and inclusive and equitable practice and to serve students: NASPA, and the American College Personnel Association (ACPA). A vote to merge the two organizations failed, with some controversy, in 2011. NASPA began in 1919 as a professional association for deans of men. ACPA and NASPA differ in size of membership, and the two organizations both bring strengths to student affairs as separate organizations. These associations collect the best practices and emerging works of staff and administrators who work for student affairs in higher education. Their work centers the student experience, and their goal is to best support the staff working in this field in order to best serve students. The types of individuals that might join this association include advisors, retention specialists, enrollment managers, individuals working in racial and ethnic minority support services, coaches, housing and residence life professionals, and undergraduate leaders. NASPA maintains a reputation for working with management and leadership professionals in the field, including chiefs of staff, directors, vice presidents, and provosts. ACPA represents a larger number of graduate students than NASPA's membership profile does. NASPA includes over 12,000 members in all 50 states plus 29 additional countries. This field, like librarianship, contains its own professional standards, and there are focused master's degrees that individuals obtain to support the development of the theoretical and practical underpinnings of the profession. Standardizing practice across all functional areas aspires to ensure quality programming and operational baselines. Toward this end, 1979 saw the creation of outlines of standards of practice for each functional area, program, or service in student affairs on campus. This was the work of the Council for Advancement of Standards in Higher Education (CAS).

Distinct support for academic advisors is found in the professional organization, NACADA. NACADA used to stand for the National Academic Advising Association, but now it is the name of an international group and not an acronym. "NACADA is an association of professional advisors, counselors, faculty, administrators, and students working to enhance the educational development of students" ("About NACADA" 2022). This organization is the global association for the development and dissemination of innovative theory, research, and practice of academic advising in higher education. The organization hosts nearly 40 knowledge communities, each reflecting a functionality or community-based role within advising. A functional knowledge community is a task-based role in advising, such as assessment in advising, advising administration, theory, philosophy, and history of advising. NACADA holds regional, national, and global conferences. Professional regions in the United States include Canadian and domestic campuses, which come together to develop best practices and find professional development and mentoring programs.

Academic advisors and student affairs professionals can both act in an advisory capacity. Student affairs professionals can sometimes perform a unique set of functions analogous to academic departments where faculty teach for-credit courses. Student affairs professionals might teach academic courses that promote success or integrity or teach internship or orientation courses to undergraduate students within their first years, though it is more common that student affairs professionals support the student through every aspect of their student life outside of the classroom. Among advisors and faculty, there is some debate about whether academic advisors are housed in student affairs or academic affairs. The reporting lines within a campus structure and the nuances in these structures across universities may make this distinction; however, advisors may perform both academic and student affairs functions. Students are often leaving home for the first time, navigating their college experience, and running into challenges and opportunities along the way. Advisors support students navigating educational and cocurricular systems. They facilitate the kinds of cocurricular content that helps students feel connected to campus life and connected to campus staff and faculty. Specified student affairs professionals, academic advisors, work to orient students to campus, outlining their major academic requirements, synthesizing course choices with professional goals, and referring students to campus resources for internships, crisis intervention, or involvement opportunities.

Advising can take on many forms in response to the student population it is serving. Advisors can be dedicated to one major or a suite of majors but can also serve students by demographic; for example, student support services advisors work with, in part, first-generation college students of any major. Advising caseloads vary by campus and by college. There are also increasing opportunities to work across disciplines, where advisors are designing their own interdisciplinary experiences for professional development as well as student services.

Advisors listen intently to the students with whom they are working to make recommendations about where to go on campus based on the students' identities and their needs. These kinds of referrals made to students by advisors are critical to the success of the students. This is why it is vitally important to instill advisors with knowledge about current library services. That can really make a huge difference in the support and care of individual students. Advisors are then knowledgeable about the library programs and services and can connect their students to just the right person for their needs. The majority of advisors are able to meet the needs of students seeking information about major/minor/certificate changes, exploring majors, or needing referrals to campus resources. However, there are specialized advisors. Academic recovery advisors, for example, assist individuals after they have experienced a departure from the university or an academic failure. In conjunction with university counseling or offices with social work functions, academic recovery advisors may also focus on getting students back into the college or university, creating support structures and/or a class schedule that may work for them and enrolling them in coursework that will benefit their ability to succeed. Sometimes they are helping individuals work through personal barriers that are substantial and impact their ability to focus on or prioritize their work. Some of these students may experience significant personal catastrophe. Students accessing these services have multiple and competing challenges in their lives. They will have many challenges. But academic recovery focuses on systemic interventions and support for students, so there are many kinds of advisors—for example, the academic recovery advisor, who works across campus partnerships to provide curated student services. Here are several types of advisors, whom they serve, and their approaches to their work.

TYPES OF ADVISORS

- Academic Advising: Offers support and direction regarding academic, social, or personal matters, including coaching and mentoring and assistance with an academic program, such as a major, minor, or certificate

- Active Military Advisors: Assist students who are active military in completing their academic plan while also operating in service to their country

- Admissions and Orientation Staff: Offers support structures in order to help recruit and enroll potential students and then assist them in the transition

- Affinity Group Advisors: Serve affinity groups with their unique needs, some of which are mentioned on this list, though this list cannot possibly be exhaustive

- Alumni Programs: Work with alumni of the college or university to maintain relationships, build a fundraising base, and offer support and programming for alumni

- Career Advising: Helps students and alumni develop career skills and translate those skills to experiences, and assists students in obtaining employment
- Campus Safety: Assists with matters concerning possible policy violations such as behavioral conduct, safety, law enforcement, and academic integrity
- Counseling, Wellness, and Clinical Health: Create support structures throughout the health and wellness spectrum, from assisting with nutrition choices to providing counseling
- Disability Centers: Serve individuals with disabilities in obtaining documentation as well as in requesting and receiving accommodations
- Engagement Professionals: Create opportunities for meaningful community engagement such as service learning, student media, civic engagement, and student union
- Financial Affairs: Support students in the financial aid application process
- LGBTQ+ Professionals: Work with affinity groups around the shared identities of students who are lesbian, gay, bisexual, transgender, queer, and the other identities contained in the plus
- International Student Services: Engage with international students to facilitate their understanding of the college or university with unique experiences and academic support
- Multicultural Services: Engage in intersectional support strategies to assist all nondominant groups to have what they need to be successful in higher education
- Sports and Athletics: Help ensure that students participating in recreational or intercollegiate sports meet sports and athletics responsibilities successfully
- Veteran Services: Support veteran students in utilizing veteran benefits and actively navigating the structures necessary on college campuses

Other advisors are trained for the express purpose of exploration of majors. Students select majors for a wide variety of reasons and then may want to switch for an equally broad number of reasons. Advisors want to focus on helping students define what success means to them and then aptly supporting them to navigate to that success.

LGBTQIA+ support is needed on college and university campuses. The support staff for this group are highly specialized and may have advanced degrees in social work or higher educational leadership. The services provided for this important group serve to create community and also manage students in crisis. They establish opportunities and make connections to help individuals with similar identities succeed in their college career.

Universities and colleges also have staff to support multicultural student success. Their areas of expertise vary and are differentiated depending on the local needs and equity issues at each institution that they work within. As a result, the services offered are highly nuanced, as they are dependent on the cultural needs of varying groups. This is important because it points to how varied services are already provided on college campuses. Designing services tailored to meet specific needs is not uncommon. What needs to take place is an expanded understanding of needs and also knowledge of those who already may support those students. In many places, as mentioned in chapter 2, there are intersectional needs, based on a combination of class and at-promise identification.

An example of a specific need regarding class and social needs of at-promise students includes students who are also parents or caregivers. Not all universities and colleges have support staff to assist in the success needs of this group of students. More needs to be done to better support them. Some campuses may provide support for very young children by offering day care opportunities. These opportunities tend to drop off as children approach school age. As a result, this need increases over time. Many students who are parents also work full-time and juggle classwork, parenting, and careers. The individuals who work in day care and other children's educational services on campuses are great places to partner with to conduct outreach to these students.

Part of the gap in advising services includes addressing the needs of specific populations. There is room to grow in creating advising services for individuals who are student caregivers, students who have experienced trauma, and students experiencing homelessness. While there are often counselors who can assist the students by providing counseling services, trauma-informed services can be included in other roles. These skills remain an area of expertise that needs to be explored through all areas of colleges and universities, especially advising and any other service-facing role that works with students.

Another gap exists with regard to service for students with disabilities. Students with disabilities need their own types of support, and those support mechanisms vary based on their disabilities. Universities and colleges should have an accessibility outreach center designed to help support students with alternative access to resources. There will be other individuals who manage programs for individuals with a wide variety of disabilities. Faculty and staff who teach or work in special education departments also provide needed support to individuals to help them succeed.

Staff in a veteran's service role are specialized to provide advising, counseling, and career services to veterans. Student veterans are a very diverse group of individuals. Their needs are equally diverse. Particular aspects of their experiences and the financial support that funds their education, as well as the requirements of that education, are characteristics unique to the veterans and bind them together.

These groups won't be reached through traditional liaison activities falling along traditional disciplinary or departmental lines. Partnerships and collaborations with advisors can go a long way to assist these students in enabling their own success, however they define it. The staff in these areas provide a great deal of guidance to the students. They meet with all students in these populations a great deal and in one-on-one environments. The advisors have insights and knowledge about the individual students they are working with. As a result, they may be better able to reach them and reinforce some of the areas on campus that may offer more support to the students.

There are many types of advisors at colleges and universities. Some advisors focus on other specific subareas of student success, such as athletics, veteran status, and so on. Not all are formal advisors, as some are advocacy based or social work driven or are involved in advising activities related to a given major. Advocacy-based advising appointments may vary depending on the population served. Services for students with disabilities, multicultural identities, LGBTQ identities, or veteran status may provide academic advising that combines academic success resources with advocacy for resources or access. Students with these experiences and identities are often met with resistance or a lack of expertise in services across campus. Advisors in advocacy are needed to bridge the gaps between students and the services they need to be successful in college. Each group may be distinct and have separate support mechanisms. Some campuses may have them all together under one umbrella. It may take some effort to locate these groups and offices on your campus. Advisors in these areas are often called upon to train university faculty and staff to effectively serve these populations. Advising that is related to a given major can occur outside academic departments—in career services, for example—or within departments, as in honors advising, law advising, or professional development organizations such as an accountancy fraternal order advising business majors. Staff and faculty can work in a social work type of role to helps students navigate the higher education system. Showing or teaching students how to advocate for themselves with instructors, for example, is one example of this. For example, many students are not aware they can ask for extensions. Another example is that as students transition to quarantine or transition from quarantine back to courses, they might work with a dean of students office to navigate conversations with faculty and public health officials. A third example can be found among students aging out of the foster care system. This kind of advising would help affected students to navigate financial aid, build university social capital, and choose a balance of coursework.

Connecting Libraries to Student Advisors

Since they play such a key role in student success, let's talk about what it's like to create a bridge to these units and break the silos. The work of some of staff is limited to appointments, consultations, and meetings with individual students and their teams. Finding time for collaboration is not always supported. But breaking the silo can start simply. Invite someone to a quick conversation to learn a bit more about their work, and share a bit about your work and your goals. Establish in an initial conversation the shared goals you have with the other individual. Future conversations will depend on the administrative support individuals obtain from their supervisors and colleagues. They may be able to collaborate and explore ways to scale up ideas to help students succeed. Depending on our own cultural modes of communication, making time to simply talk to staff or faculty from other units can feel unproductive, and conversations may seem meandering. But spending this time may be the most important basis for a partnership, as it is in those conversations you make connections. You may need to adapt communication styles when building relationships across functional units such as libraries and advising in order to cast the widest conversational net for gathering information. It's important to listen for functional area boundaries, establish the shared goals between units, and talk about individual values apart from simply finding the time to work on a collaboration. Creating these bridges and sharing some of the seminal work from your field can fuel the work that each of you does. By sharing articles and research in this regard, it can allow time for reflection and greater conversation to determine areas of concentrated effort.

Where you take this kind of connection can be empowering for everyone involved and ideally is also empowering to the students you are working to support. Through networking and a shared understanding and awareness of services we each offer, we can then work together to design new services. This process can closely mirror a design-thinking framework (expanded on later in this chapter), but it also is very similar to how librarians would normally find an information need in their community and work to fill it. The difference is in the way that you partner and collaborate. This can be much deeper than mere understanding, becoming meaningful collaborations that identify root causes of issues and meet them. On a simpler level, because many librarians are not aware of the roles that student affairs professionals do, we can work together to partner and develop services in conjunction with one another. Where we cannot offer new singular services, we can offer parallel services.

What do we mean by this? Let's explore the concepts here. Design thinking is a process of creating innovations. The process begins with developing empathy for a group you want to assist. Following this empathy step, you define problems and needs and explore the areas of problems in a community from the standpoint of the community members. The remaining steps include ideating solutions, prototyping innovations, and testing those innovations. Through a participatory lens, you can collaborate with those individuals you intend to serve. By including them in the design process, you can ethically create solutions alongside those groups. This type of modeling can benefit students in a long-term way.

A librarian continually defines information needs in the community. In both design thinking and librarianship, one focuses on the user first, though the scope of a librarian is to evaluate from the point of view of complex information problems and needs. Design thinking is a process that follows the identification of needs, much as how librarians must identify information needs in order to fill them. Design thinking identifies steps that can help facilitate the creation of a relational transaction with users. Some librarianship has been focused on a more transactional approach, such as a reference or circulation transaction. Students come to the desk, ask questions, get their information, and depart. As the world is now very information focused and information rich, discerning truthful and helpful information is key, and the crux of that is trust. Through developing ongoing relationships with our users, we can take a more design-thinking type of approach.

Students need academic services and student success administrators to collaborate. By building relationships and identifying partnerships, staff and faculty can build new services. New services, by forming supportive partnerships, would help facilitate students to succeed and thrive including our at-promise students. NASPA is a place to go for inspiration, not only for learning about the types of individuals who work in student support fields but also for examples of powerful partnerships. Many reports and posts on its website showcase amazing collaborations that have been done on behalf of students.

In a joint report called "Powerful Partnerships," the authors write, "People collaborate when the job they face is too big, is too urgent, or requires too much knowledge for one person or group to do alone" (AAHE, ACPA, and NASPA 1998). They stress that the urgent needs of students still must be met through our shared responsibility to students. This report was written to inspire and educate on the ways to meet these urgent needs. It ends with a call to action for all of us involved in "higher education to reflect upon these findings and examples in conjunction with their own and their colleagues' experience and to draw on all these sources of knowledge as the basis for actions to promote higher student achievement" (AAHE, ACPA, and NASPA 1998). Throughout this report, there are 10 principles and examples of innovative partnerships that led to greater student achievement.

One partnership example is from Bloomfield College in New Jersey, in a program called the Student Advancement Initiative. The program creates a positive feedback loop for students to gain opportunities and then reflect on their work in a productive way. This helps model ongoing improvement for them. The initiative provides programming that generates awareness and understanding of cultural experiences, advancing students' problem-solving abilities, education experiences with science and technology, and other professional competencies. This partnership between faculty and student affairs professionals stands as a precedent for this kind of collaboration and shows that it can be successful. All partners take on their own role in the program, but they participate to perform reflection as well. As noted in the joint report, the faculty and staff delivering the services reflect on their own work with the students, who are also reflecting: "Faculty and staff participate together in 'reflective practice' sessions to improve programming and administration." Modeling reflective practice is restorative and beneficial to the employees as well as the students involved.

As this partnership grew, Bloomfield College continued to innovate within its partnerships and has further adapted and extended them. This program connects students with the East Orange Housing Authority (EOHA) to offer clear pathways to higher education to the neighborhood families served by EOHA. The Student Advancement Initiative offers courses, internships, and other experiences beyond courses to help students identify and improve in specific areas.

Such programs and initiatives begin with identifying a need. Many disciplines have a protocol for identifying and meeting needs. One protocol that has proven useful in a variety of disciplines is the design-thinking framework. Though this framework was developed in the field of engineering innovation by the firm IDEO ("Design Thinking Defined" 2022), design thinking is simple enough and broad enough to be used in any area creating user-centered innovations. Design thinking also includes steps to incorporate reflective practice along the way.

Design Thinking as Iterative Reflection

In the design of services, the design-thinking framework offers an easy-to-use step process that keeps the end user at the heart of the work. By combining what is needed and useful to a user with what is possible, staff and faculty can look holistically at their resources and design better services. User experience and design-thinking research both offer insights into how to design for users. Personas are a user-experience tool; they are fictional individuals who may use your library or college but are based on data. Using personas to guide your services is helpful. Design thinking starts with ascertaining the user's needs and gaining empathy for the user. Regardless of how you do that—whether it is with interviews, surveys, studies, or observation—gaining empathy for the user is the most important step.

The steps in design thinking following empathy development are defining the problem, ideating, prototyping, and then testing. This can occur in a repetitive cycle so that one is constantly evolving and iterating a service. Empathy is understanding users from their own point of view and trying not to impose one's own ideas on users. This can be done through an interview-style process. In the work conducted at Boise State University, at-promise students used templates on how to conduct interviews and then interviewed others who represented their audience or users. In a course called University 106, at-promise students used a guided instruction session to interview others and design new services to help support those individuals.

During the interview process, they learn what barriers students face in their success as undergraduates. The results of these interviews turn into defining a problem. Often, individuals designing services do so without realizing or recognizing the actual barriers that stand in the way of student success. By conducting research into these real needs, one can design services that meet those needs. In these courses, using these techniques, the students were then able to help identify what they needed at that time and were able to better articulate what would have been a better support.

Awareness of Services

Since the library itself is such a special place for students, and because the library is where many students come, library staff and faculty ought to have a baseline understanding of the other services across campus. Even if not codesigning new services together with other individuals, librarians ought to know about the many types of advisors and student affairs professionals on their campuses, who to refer to students to, and when to do so.

Another way to improve library services is by understanding the skills partners have. As outlined in this chapter, student affairs professionals have many skills to offer the students. Librarians can offer complementary services and skills. Cross-training allows for both groups to have a potential shared understanding of how to meet students' needs. An ongoing collaboration and partnership at the Boise State University campus involves those who manage units of academic advisors. By training them in a strategic outreach kind of way, we are better able to connect with the students we all serve. Advisors trained some library staff who work in the Albertsons Library MakerLab. Library faculty trained advisors on what topics they cover in information literacy and maker literacy. Making lends itself to student success by offering tangible, hands-on ways of creation, and through this kind of involvement and engagement, students remain enrolled at the university. High-impact practices are those which are identified to support student success. The most important work on this topic was written by

George Kuh and explains the primary types of experiences that are high-impact practices (Kuh 2008).

If library workers and advisors knew more about the content areas in one another's units, all involved would be able to boost their skills, offer better support to the students, and help them thrive. This can be as simple as suggesting that a student visit the library or visit the makerspace in the library. Advisors are often one of the only points of one-to-one contact with students, especially for those in the at-promise category. Students need to meet with their advisors in order to enroll in a new semester. This is a key area for identifying students who need additional opportunities for engagement.

Mental Health First Aid

Mental Health First Aid is a growing service being offered across the country in a variety of settings. This type of first aid is designed to address the mental aspects of a crisis instead of only the physical ones. Individuals who have experienced a significant trauma or a mental health crisis fall into the category of those who could use support. Mental Health First Aid is a course offered by the National Council for Mental Wellbeing. The course provides those who attend with an opportunity to gain skills in helping others who may experience mental health issues. The course builds "mental health literacy, helping the public identify, understand, and respond to signs of mental illness" ("About MHFA" 2022).

One area that may need to be addressed on campuses is the growing need for support for students with mental illness or mental health crises. During the pandemic, we witnessed the rise of mental illnesses due to increased isolation and trauma. Counselors who are trained medical professionals and not student affairs professionals are one group to also connect with in order to further these services. Librarians and other folks on the front lines of working with students might perceive students' needs and refer them to specific targeted counselors who specialize in these areas. For example, in the library, a student who asks to have overdue fines waived due to a death in the family may be a candidate for grief counseling.

Currently, library workers may waive such fees or not, depending on internal policies. A library worker who was trained in trauma-informed services or was aware of mental health first aid would be able to better determine if there are issues or concerns. The student could receive care and referral, depending on how the referral is done. The university would be able to reach additional students this way. Imagine, too, if social workers were more embedded in all kinds of libraries to assist with exactly these kinds of issues. In short, cross-training and working with individuals who care for the whole student would benefit our library workers but also help libraries further their student success mission.

References

AAHE (American Association for Higher Education), ACPA (American College Personnel Association), and NASPA (Student Affairs Administrators in Higher Education). 1998, June 2. "Powerful Partnerships: A Shared Responsibility for Learning." https://www.naspa.org/images/uploads/main /Powerful_Partnerships.pdf.

"About MHFA." 2022. Mental Health First Aid. National Council for Mental Wellbeing. https://www.mentalhealthfirstaid.org/about.

"About NACADA." 2022. NACADA. Kansas State University. https://nacada.ksu .edu/About-Us.aspx.

"Design Thinking Defined." 2022. IDEO. https://designthinking.ideo.com.

Kuh, George D. 2008. "High-Impact Educational Practices." *Peer Review* 10 (4): 30–31.

CHAPTER SIX

Examples of Student Success Partnerships

In chapters 2 and 3, we learned that higher education student success initiatives began in the mid-1990s. In this chapter, we will connect to that history with background on student success initiatives in academic libraries. In the following chapters, readers will learn practical steps toward building the partnerships to which they're introduced here. Understanding the background of what has been tested and evaluated is important because it can help create a mental framework about how to make decisions in partnerships. There are important models and practices that individuals have attempted. Knowing what has come before us can intellectually inform us on how to best approach building partnerships.

Though academic libraries have always been there to support students and to help them succeed, they have not traditionally been the place where student success initiatives, those designed to meet equity gaps, took place. Libraries have always been the go-to information resource for students and researchers, and now, libraries have become knowledge centers and interdisciplinary hubs focused on specific services as well as places where students study. There is much potential for using the library building to serve as an interdisciplinary hub of knowledge to assist in student success initiatives. When we compare library services to student success initiatives, we see that the main purpose of the library was to support the student experience. The resulting difference is a gap in knowledge in academic libraries on how to best incorporate student success into the services offered, in terms of helping close the equity gap. This chapter shares background on some library initiatives that have worked to bridge equity gaps, showing what worked and what didn't and offering ideas to adopt moving forward.

Distinguishing between Helping Students and Student Success

The term "student success" was chosen to refer to supporting all students and addressing equity gaps among underrepresented minorities and key populations. Using this term in higher education signifies an acknowledgment by higher education institutions of their responsibilities to students. Student success initiatives are those that attempt to improve long-term outcomes for students in key populations.

As universities and colleges admitted new groups of individuals, including those which had not been admitted before, each group needed different services in order to succeed. The same services that support one group may not work to support other groups. Within this book we do not argue that higher education and academic libraries had not previously been supporting student achievement and helping all students, and especially key populations, to succeed in their goals. Indeed, these supports have existed for students, staff, and faculty at their respective institutions and beyond. However, the student success initiatives we're discussing are specific and targeted to addressing those outcomes for specific groups of students, including those who had not previously been admitted into the university. As a result of this potential conflict in definitions and understanding, the first step in creating student success collaborations is establishing a shared working definition within an institution.

Defining Student Success

Many units and departments in the academic university and spectrum of colleges define student success in different ways. Possibly, some units have not taken the time to define this for their students, while others have. In some cases, the way a department or unit might think about student success may need to be updated to reflect our current learners and researchers. How we define who our students are, and subsequently how we serve them, must be tied to how they learn. In this connection, one can find what success means to students. Defining this is critically important to best serve the students. Services and delivery methods ought to align to the services of a university unit, including the library. Indeed, in part, that is what accreditation standards provide—a mechanism for ensuring that students who enroll will succeed once they leave the university setting.

Academic Library Directions in Student Success

At the current moment, academic libraries are bringing in student success initiatives. Three excellent summaries of the current status include an Association of College and Research Libraries (ACRL) report by researchers

Brown and Malenfant, highlighting specific action programs and collaborations that worked. In addition, Lynn Deeken, dean of arts and learning resources at Everett Community College, and colleagues have written two articles published in *Reference Services Review* on prominent student success initiatives nationwide.

Action Projects

ACRL researchers received funding from the U.S. Institute of Museum and Library Services in order to learn more about evidence-based practices as they pertain to student success. Their methodology was to select a librarian on a college campus and match that librarian to staff or faculty who work in other support areas on campus. Over the course of three years, they evaluated over 200 projects and practices used by these teams. This resulted in the creation of a rich database of information that served as the basis for their final report published in 2017.

The findings reveal that there are five different ways libraries can support student success. First, providing library instruction in courses for freshmen and new students was found to result in better long-term outcomes. Second, when students use the library services, they tend to have better grades. Third, they found that when students meet regularly with their librarians, they may develop stronger student confidence. The fourth finding, and also a key to this book, is that "collaborative academic programs and services involving the library enhance student learning" (ACRL 2017, p. 15). The fifth way is that when we partner with other groups and design better programs and services, we end up with strong student outcomes.

Using action research, the teams created unique projects and services that worked to serve the specific needs of key populations on those college campuses. Librarians and the students they serve were found to benefit from forming these partnerships. Tracking those projects and assessing the outcomes, the researchers found they did meet student success goals. As mentioned below, student success metrics are important for showing success in strategic plans and accreditation standards. When librarians embark on these projects, they create additional relevance for libraries and increase graduation rates for students. ACRL suggests using action research in order to improve student outcomes. Action research is a type of research that attempts to directly improve the situations of those in the research study, so the delivery of programs may be modified to ensure a positive outcome.

Both the research by Deeken et al. and the ACRL study found that building academic rapport was an important component in helping students succeed. This is why it is important, as stated in chapter 3, to share pieces of one's identity with students in order to make connections. In addition, revealing times of struggle and explaining or showing how a librarian overcame that struggle will also be important. Students learn based on what someone says, but they learn how to problem solve by watching someone encounter something unexpected and finding a way to work with what they find. Students will adopt and emulate those kinds of problem-solving skills. According to Deeken et al. (2019, p. 504), North Carolina State University is working to "identify both significant student populations for more focused attention but also 'pivotal moments' that will impact, in a myriad of ways, student success and inclusivity." The pivotal moments that librarians can control are any interaction with the physical library, the digital presence of the library, and any connections to the librarians outside of those two spaces, such as in the classroom or at an outreach event. From there, librarians can build on creating new services to reach other pivotal moments, such as having a presence at the campus food bank or bringing a food bank into the library. Academic rapport is key to building that sense of belonging, but there are other trends gleaned in these studies too.

Leading up to its publication in 2017, the researchers on the ACRL project, Brown and Malenfant, analyzed results of 200 collaborative projects, or action teams. According to their executive summary, "since 2013, over 200 postsecondary institutions of all types have participated in the Association of College and Research Libraries' (ACRL) Assessment in Action program (AiA) that created campus-wide partnerships at institutions to promote collaborative assessment and library leadership." All of the five ways Brown and Malenfant identified that increase student success can be applied to possible partnerships.

First, they found that students benefit from library instruction. Overall, students who participate in library instruction perform better in their courses. According to one project participant, "[Tulsa Community College] librarians learned through this project that a more college-wide and coordinated effort toward curriculum development and assessment was needed to achieve success in [library] instruction." When new students obtain that information literacy, they perform better longer term than when they do not.

Second, they found that using the library did increase student success. Using the library in this context was defined for both the online presence (digital databases and the website) as well as physical building services (circulation, study room use), and those that are both online and face-to-face, such as library instruction. Those engaging with the library in those ways were correlated to have better retention and grades than those who did not. While most of these projects did focus on library instruction, they also improved the methods of collecting student success data overall.

A third way is that students meeting with their librarians can improve student confidence. Partnerships with other units on a college campus can increase the visibility of the library's offerings. Staff and faculty working with students can explain the library services to the students and improve the chances that the student will go to the library. If partners are aware of how to book time with librarians and ask for help—which could consist of librarians modeling the use of services and explaining when they might be used—this can increase the chances of at-promise students using the library.

A fourth method involves generating collaborative programs that meet unique needs of students to enhance their learning. Those unique partnerships that create new services are explored in very practical terms throughout this book. The services can promote student engagement and student learning and ultimately can improve services. The fifth way is that when we partner in such a way to make iterative changes to services, student outcomes are improved.

Accreditation and Student Success

Accreditation agencies focus on student success metrics, including retention and graduation rates. There are many other ways to consider student success. Accreditors are advising in two significant areas of priority: bridging the equity gap and enhancing student success. This may lead our institutions toward transformational change. Students are the core individuals we serve, and they are the consumers of the library.

It's important to think about the different populations of students who have participated in the university over time. Whereas in the past, the admissions process served as a gatekeeping process, and by and large still does to some degree, the individual students in the university setting are more diverse than ever. As a result, traditional methods of programs and services do not serve all of our students. The problem with this is that, by and large, a huge percentage of students fall into the spectrum of feeling marginal rather than mattering or belonging (Schlossberg 1989). The goal is to create programs that help support and empower all populations in feeling as though they matter to the college or university in which they are enrolled. Environment and conditions may cause all students to feel as though they matter or belong at different times, but services must be framed in a way to continually reiterate that students do belong.

Student success and the assessment of academic library value are defined differently at different institutions in part because there are no clear measures of student success in academic libraries. Academic libraries have made strides to incorporate student success into their strategic plans, their goals, cross-cutting working groups, and assessment plans. A variety of researchers and practitioners have tried different methods of assessing this kind of work. As key populations vary from institution to institution, it can be difficult to track. Two trends can give us insights about how to assess student success.

It is accurate to assume that individuals who enroll in a college or university intend to graduate from the institution. Graduation rates and retention rates tell specific stories and show that the result is that not everyone meets their goals. Student success rates can be tracked to specific demographics to determine which populations of students are graduating and which are not graduating. Analyzing that level of data across institutions can tell a lot about the key populations that need specific support or require additional services. Each of those populations may need additional support, different support, or services geared to help them succeed. The stories of each individual and group will differ depending on local conditions and needs. Library workers can learn about these key populations and work together with individuals who work with those users to better support them. Success for each individual and each group may be defined differently.

Another trend is that accreditation institutions are creating more student success standards and lessening the number of library or information standards. The Northwest Commission on Colleges and Universities (NWCCU) changed the standards from 2010 to 2020. In 2020, the standards include only one library-related standard. The expectation is that libraries will work to embed themselves into the rest of the work taking place on college campuses. The sole library standard remaining is: "Consistent with its mission, the institution employs qualified personnel and provides access to library and information resources with a level of currency, depth, and breadth sufficient to support and sustain the institution's mission, programs, and services" (NWCCU 2020). The 2010 standards included four library-related requirements, and libraries were also mentioned in two other standards. This change reflects a transition point. It's imperative for accreditation for libraries to make a switch to support student success by collaborating to support this mission. There are more reasons beyond these two trends, such as the intentions and goals of students and the accrediting bodies shifting to student success to focus on graduate and retention rates as a shared metric for success.

Those who earn postsecondary degrees do go on to have better health outcomes, increased civic engagement, and job attainment in areas they want to work within. Students may define success in any of these ways, even if they don't define graduating as a part of their success. Reports of their satisfaction and their self-defined attainment of success may be the most useful metric to follow, though that is not an easily obtained statistic. Persistence rates may also be an accurate measure of value for student success since there is a strong tie and correlation between retention and graduation and meeting one's own personal goals.

States, colleges, libraries, and individuals ought to look at individual demographics to analyze who is being retained and who is graduating. Looking at the demographic data to analyze racial disparities and equity gaps will help us see local gaps and opportunities for library engagement. However, there are limitations to this approach, since the responsibility for student success could be attributed incorrectly to the individual rather than to the institution. Here are some examples.

In looking at the data of which students are using specific services, one may find that there are disparities in who is using which ones. For example, if in evaluating who is using the chat reference tool, it's determined that a majority of students using that tool are white, and it does not reflect diverse users, librarians can reach out to affinity groups and let them know that the service exists. Librarians can create a task force, or a focus group, and provide funding to individuals, who will share their insights as to why individuals from other demographics are not using various resources. Those kinds of insights can be a true gift. Individuals may point out that the paintings or posters in a specific service area of the library do not depict diverse groups, that there is no diversity among staff and faculty, or that Black, Indigenous, and people of color (BIPOC) are treated differently in that space. Fortunately, these are all things that can change.

Collecting data regarding LGBTQIA+ students' use of services can be difficult due to what kinds of data are collected at an institution. It may require research or focus groups to determine. The book *Queer Data* by Kevin Guyan (2022) explains a bit about the history and absence of LGBTQIA+ data.

Demographic data may be lacking. This absence of data is an invitation to engage with that population in real and authentic terms to seek out information about what the library means to them. Historically, "when people we might now describe as LGBTQ were counted in datasets it was often a result of observable actions understood as criminal (including male same-sex activities and cross dressing), information bodies and minds were thought to provide about illness or disease, or as a means to confirm differences and cement the privileges of the majority group" (Guyan 2022, p. 29). As a result of this history, it may be challenging to collect data on this population, including that some of these stereotypes persist in our current culture. Bringing a focus group together, or partnering with a gender equity center or an LGBTQIA+ group, can help librarians learn about anecdotal and qualitative data that can inform new practices. From these kinds of focus groups, one can learn that the bathroom may be hostile or that individuals experience being treated differently or that the library uses a student's deadname. This is important data that libraries can collect once they learn of the need to do so, but the absence of such data means a librarian must seek it through qualitative means.

Demographic data can be found in other areas that result from socioeconomic impact. In these cases, students may report they do not have access to resources that other students may have. These barriers may be the result of information tools or the lack thereof. One example may be that students may not have access to the internet at home. Libraries can partner with information technology services at their institution to check out internet devices or provide methods of obtaining broadband in other ways. A longer-term strategy can be to lead and participate in regional movements to improve public broadband.

Another example may be that students may not have the time, resources, or ability to collaborate on group work where they live. Libraries may be able to assist in this by looking for ways to provide satellite information creation areas or by creating/improving hyflex spaces within the library to allow for remote and face-to-face collaborations.

There may be some assignment-collection efforts at your institution that look at what kinds of projects faculty require their students to create. If a certain number of students need to use special equipment to do so, the library can offer to check out such equipment or provide spaces in which to access these tools. Creating a data visualization space is one type of solution that many interdisciplinary students can utilize.

Dr. Christopher Nellum is the deputy director of research and policy at the Education Trust. He writes and presents about how not all students define success as their grades. Nellum's research points to how common it is to attribute equity gaps to individual students. He posits how important it is to reframe and select the right words. This is because Nellum believes that institutions are responsible for student success. When individuals or institutions insist that a student is not succeeding, some imply or state outright that the student did not try hard enough or perhaps that the student does not belong at the institution. Overall, taking into account the responsibility that institutions have to support all students by improving programs and services is key. Deciding which metrics and definitions of success to monitor and track will help all collaborations and initiatives to move forward. Once that has been accomplished, it's important to collect more data and think about which tasks and goals a collaborative effort would want to accomplish together. We now present some examples of ways academic libraries have tried to support student success.

Student Success Partnerships with Student Affairs

Academic libraries offer collections and services to help with information, but there is still much work for academic libraries to do to support student success. Though student affairs professionals have existed on college campuses since 1640, collaborations between libraries and student success/student affairs professionals are still few and far between. Many individuals do collaborate to generate specific events or to fulfill a specific need, but student success involves much more than this. Through the process of identifying or uncovering what student populations believe their needs to be, learning what success means to them, and building new services, any academic library can begin to contribute to student success writ large. There is some history on these engagements in the published literature. Though it is common for academic librarians to partner with faculty, or have official liaisons to faculty, it seems less common to find them designing services and workshops with student success administrators or student affairs staff. Though these programs and services may not be as academic in nature as direct instruction in a class or classroom setting, the lack of formality in these kinds of support structures may offer greater success for the students in the long term.

Library workers have tried to form some partnerships and establish some programs in order to enhance student success, with a variety of outcomes. One of the first waves of student success partnerships would be best illustrated through the trend of addressing students' first-year experience. These would include special programming for students that connects to their first year on campus, including the APT program in the article by Holmes and Lichtenstein that we discuss later in the chapter. Let's consider this from the point of view of a student and their experiences.

Students sometimes face housing insecurity, have caregiving responsibilities, and have multiple jobs. Some of the literature on this topic addresses symptoms of systemic barriers. For instance, these could include providing students with nap rooms, which is a symptom of housing insecurity. While it is important to provide students with places to sleep and libraries ought to provide many nuanced spaces for students, there may be higher priorities students want to address, such as obtaining affordable housing. Perhaps what is called for instead is advocating for students to challenge the systems they face, helping them navigate the systems to locate housing, and doing this while helping them remain true to themselves, without sacrificing who they are as individuals. What this means is that students want to remain connected to their community. If housing security is an issue, they will want to find solutions that help them remain their dignity. The creation of spaces may do something to challenge the inequities these students face, in this case unaffordable housing, though sometimes such efforts may serve as a balm that treats the symptoms rather than the cause. Creating specialized spaces for students that address secondary or tertiary effects of student success but do not directly address the students' needs may not be as critical for success as taking the time to work with and partner with other groups who guide these students through direct services. Creating spaces for napping, as an example, may address a secondary or tertiary effect of a primary problem. There may be better ways to address the core issues such as creating caretaking services in the library, advocating for housing solutions, or even hiring students to work-study positions. Academic librarians may do better to coordinate with like-minded individuals to create additional services that help the communities in which they serve. Academic libraries do have an expectation of contributing to student success through their services.

There is some history of librarians and libraries partnering with student success administrators. One great example is the APT program elaborated on below. Again, it's important to remember that librarians and libraries have always been present for student success in the past by building collections within the library, selecting databases, and providing instruction and services at the reference desk. All of these were in direct support of students, many of whom were unable to access authoritative information in any other way. This is still incredibly important, and it absolutely is tied to student success. As the number of student success administrators grows on campuses, and as the accreditation standards increase in a number of student success objectives, and as the internet continues to grow, librarians and libraries need to transition to partner with administrators to best assist our student populations.

Accreditation has been moving away from academic libraries having discreet goals and moving toward their needing to embed themselves with other areas. Helping others, whether as support staff or as faculty, to achieve their goals by solving complex information problems is becoming a key area of necessity for higher education. In addition, academic libraries have struggled to communicate their value over the years. Finding the right metrics to communicate that value is complicated due to a difficulty in connecting library use to student success.

Grades and Student Success

As we explore student success metrics, it's important to learn from some key studies that help elucidate why and how some metrics may be more useful than others. Particularly, grades are often suggested as a measure of success for students. However, competency abilities, such as soft skills, may be more reflective than grade point average (GPA) is of a student's ability to succeed overall in life. As Kass, Grandzol, and Bommer share in their 2012 article about students' MBA performance, the ability for students to perform well in their careers may not be tied to their GPA but to their competencies and skills. Many individuals do equate success to grades, however, so exploring the literature on this topic will be important to learn why this is not the best metric to use to assess the success of a partnership.

Some reports and research focus on tying student GPA to success because it is easy to measure, while also acknowledging there are other ways to account for student success. Gaha, Hinnefeld, and Pelligrino's (2018) research offers a path forward to enhance student success. They suggest that creating new courses geared toward teaching students information skills will enhance their success. In this research, they discuss that tying a GPA to student success could be an important metric, though they find it not to be in their study. In some cases, library instruction was positively correlated with grades, whereas in their study there was a negative correlation, which could be attributed to students who pursue many opportunities and therefore have limited time to devote to achieving a high grade in a course. The authors also recognize that GPA is not a solid proxy for success, but it is an accepted way to mark or attribute and track success of students. They also support the notion that there are many definitions of student success, which is why this ought to be defined by each university or college, library, unit, and, finally, the individual student. Though GPA is an easy metric to locate, it may not be the best to accurately measure student success and performance.

Explorations of Multicultural Efforts in Student Success

Since the student success initiatives began, academic libraries and the staff and faculty within them have explored the value of libraries and tried to create bridges designed to improve outcomes for these learners. In 1992, in his article "Addressing Cultural Diversity in Academic and Research Libraries," Otis Chadley offers the first glimpse into how academic libraries can integrate student success. Chadley points out that one initiative to increase student success could be hiring multicultural positions. This kind of strategy, which would result in an increase of diverse collections and programs for underrepresented minorities, was true in 1992 and is still true today. Chadley states, "More research libraries need to develop a diversity or multicultural services librarian position to target traditional and special library services to diverse groups" (1992, p. 211). Library researcher Agada pointed this out as well, that one significant aspect of student success is having librarians who speak to the same kinds of cultural touchpoints that the students have experienced. Chadley states, "A culturally diverse library environment is its own best marketing tool to attract diverse groups to the library and to librarianship" (1992, p. 212). Students need to find connection and feel that they matter by having their experiences acknowledged in the classroom and throughout higher education.

Emily Love (2007, 2009) wrote about a significant collaboration designed to bridge retention issues in minority students. In two articles, Love describes that while libraries perform collection development for diversity and multicultural initiatives and hire diversity-oriented librarians, it is rare to conduct outreach to and support students from minority populations. Love outlines a step-by-step process libraries can use to develop and increase their efforts to partner with campus units that support minorities. Few libraries conduct outreach to minority students. The steps include reaching out to staff who work with minority students, building a relationship, and testing the success of that relationship by expanding the services each provide. By partnering with McNair Scholars programs and multicultural student centers on campuses, librarians offer many services to enhance student success through initially offering information literacy instruction but also by expanding into other areas. By providing outreach and marketing to minority students, these students can develop a personal relationship with the librarians and staff in the library. Librarians can also be more responsive and develop instruction sessions that are tailored to the specific needs of those groups. In this case, it may be a new pathway to develop tools that work for those students.

Several studies have linked the use of the academic library to increased retention in higher education. As Ethelene Whitmire concludes (2003, p. 161), "If academic library use can be associated with retention as earlier studies indicated, it is important for academic libraries to assist their institutions with retention rates by increasing academic library use among this student population." The example of Love's projects—to partner with campus units to provide information literacy instruction, expand on those partnerships, and conduct further collaborations—should lead those populations into the academic library. Correlation is not causation, and it is possible that individuals participating in myriad high-impact educational practices such as these would benefit all students. By offering these programs to students in populations who are not being retained so well, libraries can increase retention through outreach programming.

More research is needed to differentiate between causal and correlation connections. Marta Bladek, a librarian who researches Latino students and their uses of academic libraries, provides a great summary of studies on student success. Many empirical studies draw a connection between use of the academic library and retention, though Bladek (2019, p. 9) cautions, "It should be pointed out that the above studies do not demonstrate a causal relationship between library use and students' outcomes." Croxton and Cooper-Moore explore student success data tracking and find valuable insights. They use Tinto's social integration theory and argue that "students need integration into formal and informal academic and social systems of the university to be successful. This model holds that engagement in these formal and informal systems strengthens students' academic intentions, goals, and commitment to their institutions, making them more likely to graduate" (2019, p. 216).

This type of long-term tracking of student success through graduation rates is necessary and, again, requires resources over time. Partnerships can always assess the work to determine which particular practices enhanced retention. These kinds of studies would require a lot of support.

Love outlines seven steps to establishing successful collaborations. Starting with identifying partners, Love then recommends identifying needs. She recommends making deeper connections through this establishing of a partnership before performing as a team and assessing the work. In the following chapters, we recommend several steps that are closely aligned with Love's recommendations. First, let's take a look at some other key examples of student success partnerships in libraries.

In 1996, Barbara Holmes and Art Lichtenstein, librarians at the University of Central Arkansas, published an article about how higher education began trying to increase retention rates for freshmen and especially among minority-identified students. They saw this need and attempted to fill it. What they wrote about the program they created—the APT Program—was timely then, as it is more than 20 years later.

At the time, Holmes and Lichtenstein were exploring retention rates and found that they were lower for individuals from minority communities. Their goal was to connect library research skills to success: "While it is generally recognized that instruction in library research skills helps freshmen succeed, relatively few programs exist that target library skills programs at minority students" (1998). They also explored other options that have been suggested to enhance student success, including diversity hires: "Often when the question of how to foster library success among minority students is examined, the proposed solution involves hiring a 'diversity or multicultural services' librarian. Unfortunately, although this approach may be a good one, many libraries today are unlikely to receive funding for new positions." They also pointed out that the budgets for libraries are limited, making it harder for library staff to maintain their current services: "Many are struggling to maintain current services with existing, or even smaller, professional staff." Despite these budget issues, creating new and relevant services should remain a priority in academic libraries.

The project at the University of Central Arkansas deserves emulation at other academic libraries. First, its creators identified key populations whose graduation rates needed to improve. They then sought partnership with administration and secondary education faculty, the College of Education, the College of Health and Applied Science, and what was known then as the Office of Minority Affairs in order to assist others who work directly with those students. Creating the APT (African Americans Partnering Talent) program and the APT Summer Academy, they worked to design workshops to support those students. Through targeted instruction, the APT program delivered interactive workshops that utilized active learning techniques targeted to at-promise students. They then recommended that librarians be aware of the characteristics of the individuals they are instructing and assisting. They assisted students in obtaining information literacy skills by targeting first-time freshmen. They encouraged having patience. Understanding more about the situation and circumstances of the students in these programs, gaining empathy for their unique situations, which will differ from person to person, and helping them as best one can will assist the students in succeeding in their goals.

In this case at UCA, the library staff delivered content and shared their expertise in a new way: through partnership with specific programs. They found that APT students were performing at a higher level academically than their peers were and also that 100 percent of students who participated in this program were retained. Some key elements were addressing the unique needs of these students served through the partnership, being patient with the students, and addressing all of their needs, including making connections with other experts. While this project is worthy of emulation across the United States, libraries have explored other areas of student success since the UCA librarians' article was published, with a variety of outcomes.

Creating Space: Library Spaces for Student Success

Creating spaces for key populations is one avenue that academic libraries have taken to support student success. These projects are indirect support mechanisms; they create supports for students but may not address systemic issues. As a result, these spaces are best tied to some sort of high-impact practice such as experiential learning, interactive learning spaces, community connection, or spaces that expose the students to new, emerging technologies.

Library spaces were highlighted as student success oriented in a 2020 article from *College and Research Libraries News* (Benedetti et al. 2020, p. 274). Creative space development is specified as a significant trend in academic libraries, as a way to overcome some of the barriers many students face: "In recent years, a number of academic studies and news stories have reported on the rising rates of college students struggling with depression, anxiety, sleep deprivation, food insecurity, family responsibilities, and other factors impacting student wellbeing." Citing these specific symptoms of a systemic issue, academic libraries identify spaces to meet these needs. Libraries are seen as safe spaces that serve everyone on a college campus, and as a result, their proximity and availability are cited as reasons to use the library in this fashion. Some of these spaces are doing the important work of collaborating with individuals that offer direct services, such as "collaborating with campus partners, social service agencies, and professionals" (Benedetti et al. 2020, p. 275). Some of the spaces include nap spaces, food pantries, and more. These kinds of spaces will be more effective when partnering with staff who can help guide students experiencing these issues. Starting with the student populations, identifying the folks to partner with include conducting an environmental scan of who on campus has the expertise those students need. For example, if the students are experiencing housing insecurity, who on campus can provide expertise to assist those students?

Similarly, the authors identify an increase of students with autism spectrum disorder as a reason to create collaborative instruction spaces that offer a variety of modes of learning. These spaces include a wide variety of designs to accommodate many learning styles, from quiet to collaborative. They recommend potential ways to meet this, which are seen on some campuses now: "Implementing universally designed instruction, offering quiet spaces, providing space for autistic students to use their expertise to tutor others, offering chat reference for asking questions, and conducting campus outreach to raise autism awareness" (Benedetti et al. 2020, p. 275). Offering spaces that are designed intentionally with partners and the community being served is a good solution. Partners can offer services students need that may be tangential to the library's primary information mission but are related. When those partners connect in the space of the library, students' needs may be met there.

There is still an ongoing need to design spaces that truly accommodate the needs of homeless students. Homeless undergraduate student data were not collected or was very limited prior to 2014. Several limited studies and estimates took place between 2014 and 2016. Undergraduates who experience homelessness may be likely to spend a lot of time in their libraries and may be regulars, since they have no other place to go during the day. They may be unlikely to share information about their experiences, and libraries may not be designing spaces with this idea in mind. Researchers Broton and Goldrick-Rab have studied college undergraduates for their key piece on homelessness. They conclude from the data that there was a serious retention issue regarding material hardship: "Efforts to increase college completion rates must be broadened to include attention to material hardship and shed light on this all-too-often hidden cost of college attendance" (2018, p. 129). They state that this is not an issue taken seriously enough on college campuses. Students who may use an academic library for picking up food from a pantry or to nap in a space will likely be experiencing an overall hardship.

While public libraries have made some efforts to support the homeless populations they serve, most notably by hiring social workers to assist with this population of users, not all college or university libraries have made strong attempts to meet the needs of the homeless through the design of their spaces. Public libraries have long been attuned to the circumstances of people experiencing homelessness, but academic libraries have traditionally been less likely to design and deliver services for that population.

In the article "Going Without: An Exploration of Food and Housing Insecurity Among Undergraduates" (Broton and Goldrick-Rab 2018), it is well documented that higher education provides a primary means for individuals who want to improve their socioeconomic status. The authors write, "America's higher education system includes students from diverse backgrounds with a variety of personal circumstances. Today, higher education is one of the only routes to upward mobility for those wanting to break the cycle of poverty" (Broton and Goldrick-Rab 2018, p. 121). Despite this, the ways that colleges try to help these students are through remedial skill preparation, or programs that support them with information about how to address behavioral concerns. Few focus on housing or access to food: "They rarely focus on ensuring that students have sufficient access to food and housing despite conceptual and empirical evidence indicating that securing these most basic needs is consequential for student development and academic success" (Broton and Goldrick-Rab 2018, p. 122). Libraries are generally centrally located facilities where many students use the building to sleep, find food and water, or brush their teeth. Libraries may be able to help intervene and create dynamic support structures through partnerships. Though many libraries now house food pantries for students and acknowledge that students need places to sleep, developing programs with social workers, advisors, counselors, and other campus professionals would be beneficial. After conducting some programs and studies, one could determine which interventions help best meet students' basic needs.

In an Inside Higher Ed article by Ashley A. Smith titled "Tackling Poverty to Increase Graduations" (2018), Amarillo College president Russell Lowery-Hart talks about a policy change made to fix the university to support students. He states, "No matter what is causing our students to taste failure, they are not responsible for it. We are." Amarillo College created an Advocacy and Resource Center on campus to address poverty by connecting students to resources to meet their needs. Librarians are typically well connected and aware of many information resources on college campuses. Though resources that supply childcare, homes, and food use funds to meet students' needs, and libraries may not have those resources, there are ways to help make those connections on campuses.

Creating New Programs and Partnerships

In 2007, librarians Swartz, Carlisle, and Uyeki coauthored an article describing their research in developing a program at the University of California–Los Angeles to meet student needs by partnering with student affairs professionals. They found in this case that support staff, due to the nature of their work, were able to be more creative in meeting the actual needs of students. They articulated how silo thinking could create difficult pathways for students and that through collaboration, it can be easier to pool resources and meet the students where they are. Since the common goal of student affairs professionals and library employees is to help students succeed, the researchers found addressing plagiarism awareness among students, and academic honesty practices, to be a natural place to collaborate.

In this partnership, the shared goal was student success, and one barrier they identified was the large number of conduct violations regarding plagiarism. Through conversation, they determined that the library had a shared mission to provide education regarding how to avoid plagiarism via citing published works in an ethical way. Together, they worked to develop an online tutorial as well as a workshop designed to raise awareness and teach students about proper citation and the ethical issues around intellectual property.

Swartz, Carlisle, and Uyeki mention some key areas that helped their program succeed, including having adequate support from administrators, the resources needed to fulfill such a program, and reading the same literature that other faculty and staff are reading on college campuses. They articulate roles and specified the ways the library can assist in the successful implementation of a program. They write that collaboration is also successful when they discuss shared goals and missions: "After partners have agreed to work together, collaboration begins by finding common ground" (Swartz, Carlisle, and Uyeki 2006, p. 118). One aspect of this is to make sure to keep an open mind in collaborations so that the final product is truly developed together. This book explores and expands on many ways to effectively set roles, communicate about the mission and goals, and nurture those partnerships in the remaining chapters. That is a key aspect to successful collaborations: knowing how to develop the partnership. A lot of work in this area can be found in the area of nonprofit agencies.

Reframing Success

A key aspect of the student success missions of the programs listed here is an implication that the students as individuals need something in order that they might succeed. To connect the dots with the at-promise designation, students need opportunities to grow and reflect on their progress. Libraries need to not try to fix or resolve a situation but instead to create programs to support individuals who are experiencing a wide variety of circumstances or even biases. The programs and services need to be streamlined and marketed so that those who truly need them will be able to use them. Employees at colleges and universities are responsible for facilitating successful navigations of the systems.

What's not taking place is meeting students where they are to offer support, guidance, and help. Once that initial transaction takes place, guiding them through in a relational way and touching base to connect the students to more resources is what is called for. This is a method to help transform the lives of the students. A student named Deanna George spoke about exactly this at a Pave the Way webinar event. She spoke about how one person reached out to her to offer help. George suggested that it is important for universities to hire individuals willing to make such a relational commitment to the student and not to invest in systems that promote a transactional approach ("Pave the Way Virtual" 2021).

The future of student success initiatives within academic libraries will entail creating structures to form an equity landscape. Developing policies at the statewide level would complement these initiatives, such as affordable learning materials that highlight library resources as textbooks for courses, among other kinds of initiatives that can benefit the students. As an example, Washington State has created the Washington Student Achievement Council (WSAC). Legislation created this state agency that combines educational research for student success with participatory and action research. The agency looks for evidence-based practices that increase student success and seeks to replicate them across the state of Washington. Students serve on the Council, advise, make recommendations, and take part authentically in the research they conduct. The WSAC model is one to consider moving forward, as it is primarily student centered, student led, and selects evidence-based practices that lead to student success.

WSAC has created an equity landscape that is quite robust and strategic, with actionable directions for institutions. In the report "Equity Landscape Report: Exploring Equity Gaps in Washington Postsecondary Education," the authors review the data in persistence, retention, program entrance, and graduation (Kwakye, Kibort-Crocker, and Pasion 2020). What is hopeful is the final paragraph of the report, which states that there is a pervasive gap in higher education attainment but that there are practices that can be implemented to improve the equity and pay gaps. Those practices include, for higher education purposes, increasing the diversity and multicultural landscape so that the diversity landscape reflects students' identities; providing financial aid, especially grants; creating cohort-based learning with mentoring and faculty support; and collaborating to combine student supports across campus units. Libraries can collaborate, moving forward, to take the lead on offering these kinds of programs at their institutions and also collaborate statewide to get funding for those resources.

Academic Success Centers in Libraries

North Carolina State University has adopted a model of identifying key populations and strategically reaching out to partners who serve those groups to create and build relationships: "In support of NC State's definition and vision of student success, part of our work involves identifying key student populations, as well as pivotal moments within the student experience, to develop high-impact experiences" (Deeken et al. 2019, p. 511). The university has done a tremendous amount of work in identifying partners to work with to serve students better, one highlight of which is in the creation of the Academic Success Center.

The Academic Success Center brings in the university's tutoring services, writing assistance services, public speaking services, counseling, and advising. The mission of the Center reads, "The Academic Success Center facilitates degree completion by providing a comprehensive variety of free programs and resources that promote academic skill development and independent learning within the university environment" (Academic Success Center n.d.). Students can meet with peer mentors as well as schedule tutoring or participate in drop-in tutoring, which serves many potential needs.

At the University of Nevada–Las Vegas, the Academic Support Center offers very similar services, including having services both online and in person. In addition to those services, the library hires student staff who work alongside tutors to offer information literacy coaching as well. As UNLV is primarily a commuter school with only 6 percent of students living on campus, their demographics reflect a nontraditional population to some extent (Heinbach et al. 2019). In a study that included the Academic Success Center and that focused on transfer students, they found that students do not lack in the skills they need at college. As a result, the services offered should be highly nuanced and focused on advanced skills, which will both honor the skills they already do have while offering opportunities to use those skills and translate them to a new environment.

Throughout this chapter, we have presented a multitude of examples from the literature about what has been tested and evaluated in student success partnerships. These examples shed light on ideas of how to partner and especially how to measure success. Next, we will share, in practical terms, how to best go about applying these examples to create partnerships in your community.

References

"Academic Success Center." n.d. North Carolina State University Libraries. Accessed March 22, 2022. https://asc.dasa.ncsu.edu.

ACRL (Association of College and Research Libraries). 2017. *Academic Library Impact on Student Learning and Success: Findings from Assessment in Action Team Projects.* Prepared by Karen Brown with contributions by Kara J. Malenfant. Chicago, IL: Association of College and Research Libraries. https://www.ala.org/acrl/sites/ala.org.acrl/files/content/issues/value/findings_y3.pdf.

Benedetti, A., G. Boehme, T. R. Caswell, K. Denlinger, Y. Li, A. D. McAllister, B. D. Quigley et al. 2020. "2020 Top Trends in Academic Libraries." *College & Research Libraries News* 81 (6): 270–78.

Bladek, Marta. 2019. "Academic Libraries and Student Success: What Research Tells Us." Excerpted with permission from "Latino Students and Academic Libraries: A Primer for Action." *Journal of Academic Librarianship* 45 (1): 50–57.

Broton, Katharine M., and Sara Goldrick-Rab. 2018. "Going Without: An Exploration of Food and Housing Insecurity among Undergraduates." *Educational Researcher* 47 (2): 121–33.

Chadley, Otis. 1992. "Addressing Cultural Diversity in Academic and Research Libraries." *College & Research Libraries* 53, no. 3 (May): 206–14. https://crl.acrl.org/index.php/crl/article/view/14713.

Croxton, Rebecca A., and Anne Cooper Moore. 2019. "From Matriculation to Graduation." In *Recasting the Narrative: The Proceedings of the 2019 ACRL Conference*, by the Association of College and Research Libraries, 216–27. Chicago, IL: ACRL. https://www.ala.org/acrl/sites/ala.org.acrl/files/content/conferences/confsandpreconfs/2019/FromMatriculationtoGraduation.pdf.

Deeken, L., A. Vecchione, A. Carr, S. Hallman, L. Herzellah, N. Lopez, R. Rucker et al. 2019. "Charting a Path Forward in Student Success." *Reference Services Review* 47 (4): 503–26.

Gaha, Ula, Suzanne Hinnefeld, and Catherine Pellegrino. 2018. "The Academic Library's Contribution to Student Success: Library Instruction and GPA." *College & Research Libraries* 79 (6): 737.

Guyan, Kevin. 2022. *Queer Data: Using Gender, Sex and Sexuality Data for Action.* Bloomsbury Studies in Digital Cultures. London: Bloomsbury Academic.

Heinbach, Chelsea, Brittany Paloma Fiedler, Rosan Mitola, and Emily Pattni. 2019. "Dismantling Deficit Thinking: A Strengths-Based Inquiry into the Experiences of Transfer Students in and Out of Academic Libraries." *In the Library with the Lead Pipe.* https://www.inthelibrarywiththeleadpipe.org/2019/dismantling-deficit-thinking.

Holmes, Barbara, and Art Lichtenstein. 1998. "Minority Student Success: Librarians as Partners." *College & Research Libraries News* 59 (7): 496–98. https://crln.acrl.org/index.php/crlnews/article/view/23700/31065.

Kass, Darrin, Christian Grandzol, and William Bommer. 2012. "The GMAT as a Predictor of MBA Performance: Less Success Than Meets the Eye." *Journal of Education for Business* 87 (5): 290–95.

Kwakye, Isaac, Emma Kibort-Crocker, and Sarah Pasion. 2020. "Equity Landscape Report: Exploring Equity Gaps in Washington Postsecondary Education." Washington Student Achievement Council. https://wsac.wa.gov/sites/default/files/2020-10-20-Report-Equity-Landscape.pdf.

Love, Emily. 2007. "Building Bridges: Cultivating Partnerships between Libraries and Minority Student Services." *Education Libraries* 30 (1): 13–19.

Love, Emily. 2009. "A Simple Step: Integrating Library Reference and Instruction into Previously Established Academic Programs for Minority Students." *Reference Librarian* 50 (1): 4–13.

"NWCCU 2020 Standards." 2020. Northwest Commission on College and Universities. https://nwccu.org/accreditation/standards-policies/standards.

"Pave the Way Virtual: The Student Experience in Higher Education." 2021. Washington Student Achievement Council. https://www.youtube.com/watch?v=GKquZTbFEB4.

Schlossberg, Nancy K. 1989. "Marginality and Mattering: Key Issues in Building Community." *New Directions for Student Services* 48 (1): 5–15.

Smith, Ashley A. 2018, October 3. "Tackling Poverty to Increase Graduations." Inside Higher Ed. https://www.insidehighered.com/news/2018/10/03 /college-administrators-meet-find-solutions-reduce-student-poverty.

Swartz, Pauline S., Brian A. Carlisle, and E. Chisato Uyeki. 2007. "Libraries and Student Affairs: Partners for Student Success." *Reference Services Review* 35 (1): 109–22.

Whitmire, Ethelene. 2003. "Cultural Diversity and Undergraduates' Academic Library Use." *Journal of Academic Librarianship* 29 (3): 148–61.

PART 3

Effective Collaborations

CHAPTER SEVEN

Forming Collaborations: Steps and Processes

Forming a partnership has several key steps. Starting with identifying a need in the community you wish to serve, the steps that follow include initializing collaboration, setting visions and roles, establishing tasks, and assessing the impact. This chapter describes how to conduct collaborative partnerships within the context of higher education and relies on the literature from the health disciplines and nonprofits. Understanding that higher education has limitations and codified frameworks of operation and using literature from health and community disciplines are helpful. Community-based partnerships and action research have established best practices that show what works best in that context. In this chapter, we will also share collaboration strategies written by librarian Emily Love. Love's work (Love 2007) provides additional insights we can all borrow in our own work. In this chapter, we build upon her framework and offer additional strategies. Finally, an additional model that is useful is the design-thinking framework, originally posited by John Arnold (Arnold 1956) in his conference talk "Creativity in Engineering."

Defining the Audience

What are your passions and interests? Was there a compelling story from a student that was the impetus for you to want to do more? Think about the user groups you want to serve. Finding a reason for service is generally based on anecdotal evidence or compelled by data or a combination of both. A good way to start finding collaborators is to first identify the user group you want to serve.

In the MakerLab at Albertsons Library on the Boise State University campus, the staff and faculty have a practice of encouraging all students who have ideas to start with the user group or audience they want to serve. Using the design-thinking framework (Arnold 1956), the first step is to empathize with the individuals you want to serve. Participatory librarianship is the understanding that librarians work to facilitate conversations in the communities they serve (Lankes et al. 2007). Involving others in decision-making is a form of action research. Librarians should be aware of the groups to which they belong and whether they are a part of the community they are or not. Action research, simply described, is a framework for conducting research within the communities that can directly benefit from the research.

As an example, when defining the audience for library services, such as students who have been reinstated to a college or university after leaving and pausing their studies, one can redefine library services given their specific needs. The audience would simply be "reinstated students." Within this population they will have a number of needs, some of which stem from why they originally left the university. The barriers they encountered can relate to their needs. Students who have been reinstated can work alongside the advisors charged with this specific population. Librarians can work with both the advisors and reinstated students to conduct a needs assessment and then design new services and programs with the staff and faculty.

Finding Collaborators

In the initial stages of a collaboration, you may have met someone just by serendipity who is working to serve user groups, a specific audience, or specific students. Often these individuals can be found by attending training through centers of teaching and learning or centers of research or other widespread university training. Indeed, the best way to find those kinds of partners and collaborators is through either those trainings or larger unifying events that take place on campus. Any event with discussions that allow for informal conversations on specific topics is great.

There are more strategic and less serendipitous routes to take. Through strategic outreach, it can be easier to identify these groups. There are many units on campuses that work with individuals who have lower retention rates. When you already have an idea in mind based on the population you are trying to reach, those partnerships may be easier to identify. When you are looking to work with a specific campus population to serve an underserved group, there are natural collaborators to be found.

Start by looking for units who serve the same group of students in the audience you have identified. Multicultural centers, veteran centers, LGBTQIA+ centers, McNair Scholars, and others—all of these are examples of campus units that serve specific populations. Most importantly, the students you work with can help you find those units. If you're compelled by student stories, paying attention to the other campus units they have identified will help identify collaborators. Following the students' lead: listening to their stories and hearing their needs may showcase other services they have used. Once these supporters are identified, you can establish a connection to work with them.

Approaches to Collaborations

There are many ways to approach potential collaborators. Once you have formulated an idea, it is important that in your approach, you remain open to any and all potential ideas. The reason for this is that through an action research and collaborative process, you will work together to conduct a needs assessment, cocreate outcomes and visions for the collaboration, and refine this over time. Revising ideas is important when establishing new, high-impact educational practices and services precisely because they are new and will require several iterations to get the service just right. One way to do this is to reflect on ideas, share ideas, and consider all of the new ideas that come through conversation—an aspect of participatory librarianship.

As collaborators work together, they will explore their shared vision and shared ideas. Cocreation through brainstorming is the best way to develop new services. This process requires trust among the participants, persistence, and some comfort with ambiguity. Risk-taking is best in this context, through the initial conversations of working together. It is helpful to define in these conversations what success may look like so that the ways success is measured can also be defined. The success of a partnership can be defined uniquely by the parties involved. Frequently it can mean that the all parties believed they collaborated effectively or that each individual believed the partnership was equitable. Success can also be defined in terms of metrics or outcomes for the students. What percentage of students were retained? What percentage of students passed all of their courses for the semester of interacting with a new service or program? Defining success should be:

- Something all partners agree on
- Measurable or observable
- Reportable, or something that can be shared or discussed

Explorations of Needs

While the needs of the students should be at the forefront of the conversation, conducting a needs assessment is only one aspect of the initial discussions. With regard to the shared needs of organizational units, establish how working together will meet the strategic goals of each unit. For example, many ideas could be supportive for the students, after you've established their needs and identified their barriers. Which possible needs might fit within the realm and context of the areas you are responsible for? Are there any services that can only be provided by working together?

This can be achieved by reviewing the college's or university's strategic plan, by looking at the individual unit strategic plans or goals, and by considering the perceived needs of the students. Through brainstorming and looking at these documents, make connections that would meet multiple needs, and create a list of those. Collaborators and partners will work together to validate these ideas through conducting a needs assessment.

Conducting Needs Assessments

While there is a large deal of literature on the topic of needs assessments, and the authors encourage the reader to explore as much as possible, for the purposes of these collaborations, we are looking for a simplified process. A needs assessment can start with reviewing the existing data that are already collected by the units and college or university. Some universities collect information on student groups as well as their needs. If they do not, collaborators may need to collect the data and then learn from those groups what their needs are in higher education. Let's review the basics.

What are the demographics of your institution? This should be as simple as reviewing the facts page of a university website. Typically, this will be a page that lists current enrollment, enrollment statistics, and demographics. On that page, the institution will articulate the breakdown of genders, ethnicity, age, full- or part-time status, international student status, and the like. It's important to realize that every reporting dataset may define categories differently. For example, one institution may count a category "students of color," whereas others may have "underrepresented minorities." These may not be comparable groups. Looking up the exact definitions will help if you want to make comparisons across institutions. If you're unable to locate those demographics, you can take a look at the IPEDS database, housed by the National Center for Education Statistics (National Center for Education Statistics n.d.). Looking up each institution, you can take a look at the demographics, including retention and graduation rates.

Oregon State University, for example, maintains a report of enrollment statistics by year (Oregon State University 2022). The reports they showcase are very detailed and elaborate a breakdown by college and major. Still, for an OSU researcher, not all needed data may be available on this site. It may be necessary to contact the institution's research center to try to find more information and data on the audiences you're trying to reach. IPEDS and facts-and-figures pages are not the only place to look, however, before reaching out. It's important to recognize the institutional research unit as a partner too. The unit may be able to connect you to the datasets that would be useful so you don't need to start from scratch. Other key, federal data collections to take a look at include the National Survey of Student Engagement (NSSE) data and the National College Health Assessment (NCHA). Both datasets can tell you a lot about key demographics and help you develop an understanding about themes affecting the students at your institution. For example, the Boise State University NSSE data is published and contains a great deal of information about students, what they're experiencing, and what they have reported about their mental health, physical health, and more (Boise State University 2022a, 2022b). Homeless students, however, are a difficult demographic to gain true numbers on, though the IPEDS NCES data does collect on this. The NCHA data, however, can tell you about the levels of food security at your institution. Students experiencing housing insecurity is a great example of the kind of research that may need to be undertaken by a set of individuals at your institution by conducting a study of current students.

If you are not able to locate the information you need, you can develop a research study to target your key demographics and learn more about their needs and ideas. You may need to conduct research in order to understand the students' needs as the data may not exist otherwise. The purpose here is to learn as much as possible about the audience you are trying to serve. This helps develop empathy and a broad understanding of the groups you are focusing on.

After identifying the audience and collecting the existing data about that population, it's important to understand what they need in order to be successful. This often means acquiring both quantitative and qualitative data. For example, some universities may collect data about students who are parents, who are experiencing homelessness or have housing insecurity, who are food insecure, and so forth. In conducting a needs assessment, finding existing data is the first step, but conducting surveys and focus groups should follow this collection in order to determine the gaps in services.

Cross-Training in Collaborations

There is one huge benefit of collaborating, whether or not a new service is created. This is the cross-training that comes from collaborating, which leads to a greater understanding about the skills and services involved in one another's units. This knowledge benefits the students and the institution. The mere act of engaging in professional and personal growth through collaborative learning can be one definition of success. This learning demonstrates growth and reflection. Imbuing a partnership with reflection is a great plan from the outset. Doing so alongside the students is a best practice to demonstrate learning. In considering how students learn best, experiential learning and modeling can reinforce the material they are learning. In short, if they see educators and leaders reflecting, they will reflect as well.

There are intrinsic and impactful reasons to demonstrate and conduct learning alongside the students, but also, the content acquisition can remarkably assist students. One key metric, tracked by NSSE data, is whether students feel like they belong. Though this can be an issue of mattering to the individuals on campus, it can also be about whether they can navigate systems of higher education. By cross-training and acquiring new content area skills, staff and faculty can learn how to address certain key issues and make more informed referrals. This can be as simple as training students on how to conduct informational interviews, a role of the career center.

Imagine students who share with you that they want to go into a certain field but don't know how to go about it. For example, they want to work in writing marketing information for publishing companies, but they don't know anyone in that field. You may want to suggest they conduct informational interviews, something the career centers on campuses would be well versed in and able to train and educate students about. If the students are in the library and sharing information about their dreams, the librarian or library worker can likely provide baseline information and then make an informed referral. Taking that a step further, the library and the career center could partner to offer services on how to research businesses in their chosen fields and then how to conduct informational interviews.

In this cross-training model, the library and a collaborator unit would train one another on the skills from their units. Providing training to entire units or groups will increase the understanding and knowledge of the other campus entities. This not only creates awareness of campus services but can also make it much easier to identify the gaps in services.

Setting Expectations

Within the first brainstorming meetings, discussing roles, expectations, goals, and outcomes are great. Knowing that this will just be the first time these ideas are discussed will help a great deal. As a result, the stakes will be lower, and the collaborators will learn more about one another and how to navigate partnerships. Over time, and as the partnership gains administrative support, goals, roles, outcomes, and tasks assigned will change and improve.

Overview of the Collaboration Process

Step 1: Identify Audience

When we start to care about a particular problem, it's generally because of data or a compelling story. When considering the barriers, it's important to start with defining whom it affects. Developing a strong understanding of who may be impacted by particular barriers is important. It may be, too, that individuals would have a specific group they want to work with but are not aware of the barriers they may run into. In either case, developing those audiences in detail is the most helpful first step.

Here are some examples of effective audience statements:

- First-generation students
- Students without parental support
- Black students
- Students from a particular city, town, area, or type of region, such as rural or urban
- Homeless students
- Students with caregiving responsibilities
- Students who work full-time
- Students who are veterans

Step 2: Environmental Scan

After identifying this audience, conduct a basic search assessment of which campus units and external partners may already serve this audience. It's important as well to identify, if possible, any existing datasets that survey these demographics.

Step 3: Establish Connections with Collaborators

There are a number of ways to meet potential collaborators. For one, an individual with a well-established network may know individuals working in those units. In the case where that does not already exist, one can reach out to unit heads or attend events where like-minded individuals might be. An example could be attending training on how to serve first-generation students. Meeting with the potential collaborators is the next step, once the initial connections have been made.

Step 4: Identify Needs

Not making assumptions about the groups you intend to serve is crucially important. In this step, the collaborators will collect data and conduct needs assessments, where appropriate, about the barriers and needs facing the students you have identified. Your ideas about their needs may not match the needs they identify. It is important to remain open to such new information and not become prescriptive.

Needs assessments are systematic methods used to discern characteristics of a population. In this case, a needs assessment is conducted in order to learn about specific student populations' needs. Needs may be unique to populations, and some needs may be shared. A combination of looking at existing data with conducting research studies is a necessary part of this step. Needs assessments begin with collecting existing data. Creating surveys and focus groups are ways to document and learn about the needs of key populations. Identifying the gaps in the services provided is one important purpose in the needs assessment for at-promise students.

Step 5: Brainstorm Possibilities

Generating ideas about what is possible and aligning those ideas with what is needed is a very satisfying step. This is where the prework begins to serve the collaborators effectively. In these conversations, you will begin to see where there are gaps in knowledge, and collaborators may need to gather or conduct additional research. These conversations will ultimately shape how the services may look and will establish the vision for working together.

Step 6: Unit Support

Once the collaborators have generated an idea and have supportive data to back up the idea, it's time to bring the suggestion to administrators. Sometimes they need additional outcomes, costs, or more data. We recommend bringing ideas earlier, to find out what additional information is needed before doing more work. Once you know what is needed, work with the collaborators to gather more insights and projected costs to deliver a formal proposal. Initial buy-in is needed before the idea progresses.

Step 7: Finalize Plan

Finalize the plan, including tasks, roles and expectations for what will be delivered and when. Take this plan to colleagues and administrators for feedback, and revise where appropriate.

Step 8: Implement

Implementing the ideas should go best when all of the previous steps have been followed. By addressing the new ideas with others, determining the impact, and soliciting feedback, implementation can go very smoothly.

Step 9: Assess

From this point, after the service has been delivered, it's crucial to collect data. This data can be formal and informal through verbal feedback and emails, surveys, or other research studies. From here, it's important to engage in a cycle of continual improvement, rapid iteration, and revision.

Community-Based Participatory Approaches (CBPAs)

Health disciplines have found community-based participatory approaches (CBPAs) to be effective in solving community issues and meeting community needs. In these processes, multiple agencies collaborate with the community in order to form an effective practice of improving community health. Because of this success, they've been able to consider research-based best practices about how to collaborate and communicate, including establishing, forming, and sustaining partnerships. This approach will be discussed throughout chapters 9, 10, and 11 on how to grow and thrive in a partnership.

In the next chapter, we will explore how and why makerspaces and services with emerging technologies fit well into this framework. Not only are they new library services being offered, so they are a natural fit, but they need a continual process of evaluation. Additionally, working with emerging technologies in an applied manner is a high-impact educational practice that can serve students well through gaining new skills and additional opportunities.

References

Arnold, John E. 1956. "Creativity in Engineering." *SAE Transactions* 64: 17–23.

Boise State University. 2022a. "National Survey of Student Enrollment (NSSE)." Institutional Research. https://www.boisestate.edu/ie/surveys/nsse.

Boise State University. 2022b. "Wellness Facts and Figures." Wellness with BroncoFit. https://www.boisestate.edu/broncofit/wellness-facts-and-figures.

Lankes, R. David, Joanne Silverstein, and Scott Nicholson. 2007. "Participatory Networks: The Library as Conversation." *Information Technology and Libraries* 26 (4): 17–33.

Love, Emily. 2007. "Building Bridges: Cultivating Partnerships between Libraries and Minority Student Services." *Education Libraries* 30 (1): 13–19.

National Center for Education Statistics. n.d. "IPEDS: Integrated Postsecondary Education Data System." Accessed July 1, 2022. https://nces.ed.gov/ipeds/use-the-data.

Oregon State University. 2022. "Enrollment Summary—Fall Term 2020." Office of Institutional Research. https://institutionalresearch.oregonstate.edu/sites/institutionalresearch.oregonstate.edu/files/enroll-fall-2020.pdf.

CHAPTER EIGHT

Emerging Technologies and Makerspaces as High-Impact Practices for Libraries

Research into high-impact practices has been trending upward since 2000, making strides to address the achievement gap. One of the biggest challenges in higher education today is to make learning and success equitable to all demographics and students. In this chapter, we explain what high-impact practices are and design-thinking methodologies that can be used to create new services and teach students. We then discuss emerging technologies and other trends in terms of what's happening in academic libraries. We explore how academic libraries can offer emerging technology services that may correlate with high-impact practices. We focus on makerspaces, as they are one trending support structure in academic libraries. Libraries with makerspaces already are building a community hub for students that can and should be used to support all students, but especially at-promise students and strivers. We share ideas, examples, and practices that can be used to counteract the at-risk phenomena and adequately support at-promise students. Throughout this chapter, you will learn about how these high-impact practices can serve to support students in meeting their goals, ultimately seeing the creative support spaces inside a library as a form of high-impact practice.

High-Impact Practices

George Kuh is an education researcher whose work is widely well regarded. Kuh defined high-impact educational practices that will actually benefit students to succeed. These practices drive students to obtain their goals, including graduating from college. They include internships, service learning, and research. In all of these practices, students are brought directly into the work of faculty and staff. Students make connections with their peers and with leaders in areas they are interested in. In these practices, students obtain skills and are also able to learn while doing. Often students are working to solve a problem. High-impact practices encourage deep learning and can be measured on the National Survey of Student Engagement (NSSE). High-impact practices, according to Kuh, must result in significant learning, increased engagement, and positive impact on underserved student populations.

Along with Kuh's work, other research indicates that student success can be shaped by having access to a community of learners who support the student and connection to a faculty member. According to researchers Bickerstaff et al. (2020), for institutions where students commute to and from campus, "faculty are perhaps the most critical stakeholder in supporting student success" (p. 7). As many librarians are faculty, and some of them teach either for-credit courses or one-shot instruction, the faculty in a library can serve to help students succeed. This can be done through the creation of experiential learning in the library. This may be through paid internships, student jobs, or the creation of experiential learning hubs.

Students also need access to opportunities that benefit them. As Carol Geary Schneider writes in her introduction to the book *High-Impact Educational Practices* (Kuh 2008), our most important challenge in higher education is to bridge the gap and help "America's extraordinarily diverse students reap the full benefits—economic, civic, and personal—of their studies in college" (Kuh 2008, p. 1). The research Kuh conducted depicts how students most in need gain the greatest success when educators rely on these high-impact practices. Allowing for all students to participate in such practices is key. As we explore this research, it's important to keep in mind in which ways library services will benefit students when considering these practices: Do library services currently use these practices to enhance student success? Student success is often correlated with a connection to peer groups, belonging, and connection to or relationship with a faculty member. Evaluating services with these attributes can be beneficial for students.

Active Support Strategies for Student Success

There are many practices that libraries can adopt in order to support student success—for instance, instructional practices, as described in chapter 3; and new services, as described in chapter 6. Here we dive into some of the more experiential and emerging technology services.

As we saw in previous chapters, success centers, knowledge centers, and interdisciplinary hubs can be created. In addition, librarians can create experiential learning centers in their facilities, where they can connect with students, build rapport, and help them succeed. What would be in an experiential learning center? Over time these services will change, but there are some examples, from entrepreneurial hubs to makerspaces, that one can consider.

North Carolina State University Libraries have created high-tech spaces to provide access to students and help them "impart skills and experiences that apply beyond a student's academic career" (Deeken et al. 2019, p. 510). Those spaces include, but are not limited to, a data visualization studio and a teaching lab. Many libraries add makerspaces for this purpose as well, which often include 3D printers, laser cutters, and other tools that help students apply their strengths to new technologies. Even more, some libraries check out audio and video equipment that students can check out or use in library studios. On the coding end, libraries also check out arduinos and raspberry pis, which allow students to create projects using coding and sensors. By using these new technologies, students can boost their resumes and create projects they can use for their portfolio and in job interviews.

Entrepreneurial services are another example of the kind of resources and services that can be developed for students in this realm. Some libraries have patent and trademark offices that help students protect their ideas and their work. Again, at North Carolina State University, they found that these services were only accessed within specific disciplines for students in particular majors. Now they collaborate and partner campus-wide to create an Entrepreneurship Alliance. Their focus in this area is that the librarians connect "entrepreneurship students with a broad range of library workshops, offers space for student teams and events, provides outreach, and coordinates new workshops and partnership" (Deeken et al. 2019, p. 510). Entrepreneurial skills can benefit the library staff as well as the students by cultivating a mindset that creates services to meet needs.

What's most important is that as students change, the services need to change. In addition, since a library is providing access to specific resources and technologies, as those resources and technologies change, the library must adapt as well. So we encourage librarians to use design-thinking strategies to generate new support structures on a regular basis.

As mentioned earlier, as emerging services come about and faculty learn about them, it's important to showcase learning and conduct reflection to enhance students' understanding about how to solve problems. Ongoing professional development for librarians, library workers, and faculty is crucial. "But even full-time faculty, who have access to a broader range of resources, may still have unmet professional needs related to supporting student success" (Bickerstaff et al. 2020, p. 8). Continuing to stay active and keep learning about new emerging trends will help stay connected to the students. Being able to actively converse with students about their interests will best assist workers in understanding how they can connect students' experiences to their coursework.

Design Thinking

When working to design new services, librarians would start with the needs of the students, using the design-thinking framework. Design thinking is a methodology that has existed for decades but came to prominence recently. The process originated with a conference proceeding by John Arnold called "Creativity in Engineering." Being creative in engineering pursuits, along the lines of design thinking, is for when the problems at hand are complex and broad as opposed to problems that can be solved with logic. Arnold (1956, p. 17) explains, "There are a great many approaches that can be used in arriving at a solution. The many different approaches used lead to many different answers." According to IDEO, design thinking and human-centered design is for "problems that are complex, open-ended, and ambiguous" ("Design Thinking: History" n.d.). Design thinking starts with developing empathy for the users one is designing for, examining barriers and problems in depth. This can be referred to as "luxuriating in the problem"— in other words, spending a lot of time trying to deeply understand the barriers others face. Through ideating, testing, and evaluating, one can generate a potential solution.

The process for implementing design thinking is similar to the process of designing services for student success. The processes begin with the complex problem, a problem that is broad and has multiple answers and possibilities. Through testing and evaluation and comparing ideas against data, a solution can be considered and adopted. First, define the audience you wish to design for; then work to interview some audience members to get at their specific needs. Learning about the audience you're trying to serve is important.

Makerspaces and services with emerging technologies not only reflect design thinking but also can teach design thinking as a skill to others. In the MakerLab at Boise State University, design thinking is an emerging concept that helps complement the information literacy frameworks. Students participate in design-thinking sessions where they help build a better makerspace, design for prosthetics, and design to help solve problems for other students like themselves.

Design Thinking, Emerging Technology, and Belonging Lesson Plans

When working with at-promise students, there are several ways to engage them in information literacy instruction while learning design thinking and capitalizing on their strengths. Below are three ideas you can implement in a library instruction session. Please don't stop here, however. Paolo Blikstein, a researcher at Stanford University, has helped create two ebooks called *Meaningful Making* that have hundreds of ideas for activities that combine belonging and emerging technologies (Blikstein et al. 2016). You may not find exactly what you're looking for, but it's very simple to adapt ideas in the books for any audience.

Displaying Strengths

A successful first meeting with a group of students can combine an introduction and tour to the academic library while also using emerging technologies to showcase their strengths. This activity can be adapted for both online and in-person instruction. After engaging students on a tour, a librarian can use a digital editing space such as Padlet or can use an item the library checks out or has in the makerspace, such as a vinyl cutter or a laser cutter.

Ask students to think about times they have used their strengths to overcome barriers in their lives. The instructor can share some examples. Perhaps the instructor's education was difficult to finance, so the instructor held multiple jobs while living in cooperative housing. Sharing expenses with peers and being willing to collaborate and help others can be strengths. Details about the setting and examples used can go a long way in helping students generate ideas on their own.

Next, use an image database such as ArtStor or the free database the Noun Project. If using a vinyl cutter or laser cutter, take advantage of the Noun Project's icons, which can easily be etched or traced. Ask students to find an image that relates to their strength. Borrowing from the instructor's example, you may find the image of a house or a group of people. If you work digitally, you can display the images on a shared slide, a collective notes document, or Padlet. If the work is done in person, it can help facilitate belonging to create a space that displays the item you found. Use a vinyl cutter or laser cutter to cut out the icon while teaching the student how to use that piece of equipment.

Interviewing Skills and Creating a Want Ad

In this activity, students will reflect on their experiences, learn about others' experiences, and identify ideas for areas or services on college campuses they wish to improve. This is a three-step process of instruction, brainstorming, and action.

I start by explaining that students will interview one another to learn more about their college experiences. The purpose of this assignment is to find out what students' needs are, which ones have been met, and which have not been met. Next, guide the students first by explaining interviewing as a technique. In the workshops we conduct, I use this language: Interviewing is a technique to use to learn more about the individuals for whom you are designing services, prototypes, or products. Think of it as engaging with someone, and not a survey. Respond naturally to ask them deeper questions. Your goal is to have a better understanding of how that person thinks or feels.

Interview best practices include:

- If someone says "I think" or "I believe," ask them why they think/believe that
- Only state 10 words for each question
- Ask only one question at a time
- Wait for their response
- Ask questions that will provide for a long answer rather than "yes" or "no" answers

After providing instructions, ask students to prepare by brainstorming questions. Once they have brainstormed the questions they wish to ask, they're ready to interview one another. This can easily be done in pairs that shift after 5 to 10 minutes of interviewing. Once each student has interviewed and been interviewed three times, they all will have data. During this time, the students will have gained empathy and understanding for the individuals they are designing for—other students.

The next step in the process is to create a "job ad." The purpose of this is to help them define a problem. They will work in groups of two to four and discuss some themes from their interviews. In this process, they work to generate an understanding of a problem they wish to solve. The directions can be broad, such as the following: In this activity, you will create a problem statement from the point of view of those you interviewed. Design the needs of the students, or users in need, based on what they need to solve a challenge or issue they are facing. In this process, you will divide the problem into key aspects:

- Form a team of two to four
- Share summaries and stories of the users you interviewed
- Create a want ad, using collaborative decision-making to arrive at the answers

Providing a structure for a want ad can be really useful to help students formulate their ideas. Using these questions, students can begin to establish their problem statement, which will usually set criteria, much like a "job ad." These questions can include:

- What are the user characteristics? (Use adjectives.) Happy? Worried? Excited? Social? Kind?

- What are the user needs? To feel loved? To feel supported? To change their major? To have friends?
- What insights can you make? (Examples: Time with friends is important. Online social networks make it worse.)

These answers tend to form a "job description" and create the "essential duties" of what students are looking for. Students then fill out a problem statement that fills in the blanks about the type of students they are designing for and what they seek. An example might be, "Parent-students seek a quiet place to study while their kids are cared for." Another example could be, "Students who have never been in a college library before seek a non-overwhelming tour of the building." Students can create three or more problem statements. It is at this point that students start to ideate new services for themselves and can start to search for comparable services.

Traditional and Emerging Library Services

It's useful to acknowledge that libraries seem to have traditional services while emerging services get brought in. It can be very challenging to introduce new services, and there can be a tension in the relationship between new services and older services due to the resources allocated to each. Even more, should a university decision-making body cut a preexisting service as a result of changing strategic focus areas, it can be difficult for folks who aren't adequately prepared to transition to the new service. From a grassroots perspective, a new service under consideration can be difficult to implement if it does not address a strategic priority; there may not be enough administrative buy-in to support the new idea. This is why evaluating new services and prioritizing student success initiatives are critically important.

In part, this is why emerging services, including makerspaces and work with other emerging technologies, need to rely on collaborations across campuses to help meet the need. They help to provide additional support, external validation of the service, and, sometimes, resources. Emerging technologies within libraries provide access, coaching, and formal instruction on creating new knowledge and information.

Open educational resources (OER) are a key area where libraries can assist faculty and instructional designers to build courses without significant textbook courses. Librarians can help faculty locate OER, which are freely available, high-quality texts that can be used in place of traditional textbooks. In some cases, faculty work with students in an experiential way to have students write a textbook for the course and then publish that as an OER textbook. Library resources, such as ebooks and articles, can also be used like

OER, because they are accessible to the students: their fees are already embedded into their tuition and fee structures. The purpose of using OER is to lower the costs associated with taking courses.

Z-degrees are zero-additional-cost degrees that offer no fee-based textbooks or course requirements for all courses in the degree. In these programs, which are an emerging trend, students would take all required courses without having to purchase a single textbook. Z-degrees have the potential to truly equalize access to degree pathways.

Emerging Technologies in Academic Libraries

Academic libraries have increasingly been including emerging technologies in their facilities. Computer laboratories became a standard to provide access to digital catalogs, and over time, to the World Wide Web and databases. Students began to increasingly rely on information on the internet rather than on the library shelves, and computers became the standard for finding information. Whether students find that information on the free web or in databases is another matter, but that they gain digital skills in using the digital catalog and computer systems to access information is key. As a result, libraries became hubs of digital literacy.

Libraries have democratized access to information and emerging tools. Tools that help us engage with and use information can often now be found in a library. They include items that individuals may not have at home and that students may not be able to afford: WiFi, printers, photocopiers. Some libraries have created music studios for their students—again, this is all going back to the needs of the population you serve. Checking out audio and video equipment also provides access to much-needed emerging technologies.

Collaboration with Emerging Services

Collaborations between units on a campus can seem challenging; however, this strategy may be the best way to embed student success practices into existing services. By focusing on shared user needs, units can connect two processes together into a shared service that will allow students to have their needs met in better ways. Through a cocreation process, teams that include the library and other units can work together to share resources and produce a service better than the one created individually.

When considering how to embed collaboration and student success into existing service, the challenges can seem daunting. Sustaining any library service while navigating budget constraints can be difficult. When those services grow due to high demand, this growth can create additional difficulties due to available resources. Relevance of library services is very important, and so library services must always iteratively improve. Working to consistently improve services will help make the services more relevant. Coordinating with other units, it's easier to share resources to get to a better result. Together we can imagine capabilities beyond what we can accomplish alone. The shared resources will come into play here to reach a destination of student success.

Experiential Learning

Emerging technology hubs, makerspaces, and the like can create excellent experiences for students. By participating in experiential learning spaces, students can add to their resumes and portfolios and use examples from these spaces in job interviews. They are a great fit for all students but especially for at-promise students, who come to colleges and universities with a diverse set of experiences. Experiential learning allows students to become engaged, either in projects (formal coursework or informal projects) or by having internships and jobs in these spaces. The insights they gain from leadership positions and making things serve them well in a makerspace.

Some of the skills to be gained through prior experiences include, but are not limited to, project management, leadership, rapid iteration, prototyping, problem-solving, and empathy. At-promise students may gain these skills in working part-time jobs, caregiving, repairing things, or building something from scratch. Making and creating often lead to multiple failures before they succeed. In a makerspace, it's important to demystify making by talking about other experiences and how they translate to making and research.

One way to do this quickly is, by way of introduction, asking all participants in an instruction session to talk about the most recent thing they made. Even when it's something like coffee or a sandwich, librarians can discuss how there was a set of steps that went into that process. This acknowledgment can help connect students to the type of learning that takes place in a makerspace. Other students may have had experiences taking apart and/or rebuilding motors, erecting structures, and making greenhouses. These experiences are also valid. By talking about these experiences, honoring them, and celebrating them, a librarian can help students connect to academic research.

Makerspaces and Experiential Learning

A great deal of research involves having ideas and testing them via the scientific method. By showing students how their experiences in a makerspace may connect to research strategies, they can feel grounded in this kind of work. One anecdote that can be especially helpful is asking about a time someone made cookies and it didn't work. Sometimes they were left in the oven too long and burned, or they were not left long enough and didn't harden. Sometimes a person may use salt instead of sugar. In all of these cases, it's easy to connect the kinds of steps involved to 3D printing.

Since 3D printing relies on a set of steps, and a specific process, including setting selection, cooking is a great analogy. As 3D prints fail or succeed, students can create their own research logs to track what settings they chose, what worked, and what did not. In that way, you can train them to become researchers and see how their experiences directly translate to knowledge.

Using Makerspaces for Celebrations

Campuses celebrate commencement, the graduation of students from a university, and convocation, the entry point of a college career. Librarians ought to be involved as much as they can in these important rituals and celebrations in order to make connections with students. Makerspaces can also serve a role. By creating a piece of the experience, such as 3D-printed logos for students, or laser-cut items in their makerspace, the library can help connect students to the services they provide. Celebrations are important for assisting students with feeling like they belong and that they matter. There are a few ways makerspaces can help facilitate this kind of connection.

At the start of every semester, there are some important events for welcoming students to campus. While it's important to be present to help facilitate information services, the makerspace can also help provide and mark a welcome for certain students who may feel marginalized on the college campus. Those who are interested in emerging technologies and 3D printing can sometimes feel isolated. More research needs to be done on this. Makerspaces, once students find they exist, can help students who feel marginalized in other areas find opportunities in the library. Events from the library's makerspace on the campus can help solidify that connection. Students who make things in their home lives, whether for fun or out of necessity, may find comfort and feelings of belonging when they see any kind of do-it-yourself activities. Tie-dyeing shirts, making buttons, zine making, 3D printing, and potting succulents into 3D printed pots are all activities that can attract students. Creating celebratory items can really help the students mark their time in college.

Setting up makerspace training and education by using a badge platform can also be effective. In makerspaces, students need to learn about use and safety pertinent to each piece of technology. If students obtain a badge or a certificate for what they have learned, they can showcase that in their portfolios and commemorate the kind of learning they did at the makerspace. One badge could be to honor prior learning as well. Another badge can use authentic assessment to create a video or documentation about what they created in the makerspace. These badges can be used to show their knowledge when applying for jobs. One badge that can be given is one that showcases a great failure. There are some failures that are so spectacular that they help inform everyone using the space learn something new about the limits or possibilities of the technology. Commemorating this can be really important and honors the way students explore a lot in research before succeeding.

There is a lot of research on microaggressions, but one way to combat them is through the practice of microempowerments. Microempowerments are interpretive statements that makerspace leaders or faculty can make to describe what the students achieved and show how their achievements connect to prior learning and/or new opportunities. By stating how their projects honor what they have learned, students can feel as though they matter. Celebrations to commemorate learning can be small, but they can go a long way in making a difference. When students see how their experiences help them build knowledge, it can change their perspectives about themselves.

Emerging Technologies and Makerspaces as High-Impact Educational Practices

Makerspaces are unique spaces on college campuses that provide special opportunities to all students. Makerspaces in academic libraries serve everyone on campus regardless of their major or discipline. They also attract individuals who don't often find a place for themselves anywhere else on campus. Makerspaces reflect emerging technologies and also traditional technologies, such as sewing machines or hammers and drills. Individuals who have worked on practical projects or had experiences in other working environments, and those who are in nondominant groups, often find the makerspace to be like a second home. They also attract individuals who have ideas for prototypes, new services, and products they want to invent. It's a great place for folks with passions to make their ideas come to life.

It's important to recognize that the nature of the makerspace is to work with emerging technologies. As a result, those leading those spaces should also be leading by example through the ongoing learning processes of acquiring new skills. According to makerspace pedagogical founder Seymour Papert, teaching is often a product of showing others how we troubleshoot and learn for ourselves. We teach a process of how to learn rather than what to learn (Papert 1972).

Making and makerspaces can be a highly personal resource. Makerspaces honor experiential learning. In this way, prior learning making and creating are also honored in such a space. Individuals may have had a wide variety of experiences. Different individuals will have experiences tied to aspects of their identity. Students who fixed things, made things, or had part-time jobs all bring with them experiences that set them apart. These technology, leadership, and project management skills support the students in gaining access to more opportunities in higher education. Makerspaces are one of the many places to help students make that connection.

Many academic libraries contain makerspaces. Makerspaces are well poised to help facilitate student success. As Kuh writes, "The nation's future, employers contend, depends on the United States' ability to help a much larger fraction of Americans achieve high levels of knowledge and skills" (Kuh 2008, p. 5). In his work, Kuh outlines several key aspects that connect learning outcomes to high-impact practices. Makerspaces are one of the areas in a library that can help individuals find greater opportunity. Kuh acknowledges that not all students who are in college today would have applied or been admitted to college in the past, meaning that we are letting in more students, all of whom come from differing backgrounds. He writes, "How do we dramatically lift the levels of college engagement and achievement for students who, two decades ago or more, would not have been in college at all?" (Kuh 2008, p. 7). Libraries and their existing services can meet the needs of students, but to what extent do existing services "dramatically lift" engagement with students, like Kuh suggests? A dramatic lift would assist current students in higher achievement. Is it possible that makerspaces or emerging technologies can assist with this? The authors believe that makerspaces in academic libraries are one area that can offer deep, authentic engagement with library staff and faculty and students.

Facilitating new knowledge creation in a makerspace is meaningful work for library employees. Students may have project ideas or academic ideas. In a makerspace, there is generally an information need, and the employees there help coach and guide the students to solve their issue. A makerspace is a complex opportunity network full of individuals, emerging technologies, and communication. In the process of achieving their project, students have experiences that deepen their sense of social responsibility, in terms of making for the social good within the context of a university. They integrate all of their knowledge and apply it to the project, which often serves the community to some small or large extent. The students are engaged and asking big questions of one another, exploring topics interesting to them. All of these touch on some of the goals of higher education, according to Kuh (2008). Makerspaces engage and invite users in part because they provide a complex opportunity for students to engage with each other, create, and feel satisfaction from working together.

It is nearly impossible to make something in a makerspace without others being interested in it as well, based on the way the space is laid out and how the open lab functions. Simply the visibility of the space and the projects being worked on piques the interest of the other users in the shared area. In this way, the space lends itself toward the sharing of stories and ideas. Students find inspiration and collaborations. As they have conversations about their projects with one another, they tend to discuss their majors, coursework, and prior learning experience.

As students have conversations, they also learn about the ways they problem solve. They look at the problems they are trying to solve through an interdisciplinary lens. Makerspaces, because they are such shared, personal, and visible spaces using very innovative equipment, naturally help inspire interdisciplinary work and projects. When individuals find that they share passions, whether it be by type of audience or the type of barriers they are trying to solve or overcome, the students form connections. They find opportunities through a complex opportunity network that leads to faculty, staff, research projects, service-learning courses, and so on. These are more high-impact educational experiences that lead to student success. Many of the skills obtained through experiences, whether in college or outside of college, in jobs or in assisting family members, can enhance student success.

Given that libraries provide access to emerging technologies, library services must continue to do so and also meet the call for continual improvement. Library services and their employees should continually respond to the needs of the students. This in turn enhances their lifelong learning. Student success is not a metric; it's an active and ongoing iterative action.

In the next two chapters, you'll learn about specific skills to collaborate and join together with others in this kind of design. By using the core of design thinking and collaborative partnership research, there is a lot to learn about how to work together. In chapter 9, you'll learn about the sustaining of partnerships, while chapter 10 will address how meetings can operate and how to use consensus.

References

Arnold, John E. 1956. "Creativity in Engineering." *SAE Transactions* 64: 17–23.

Bickerstaff, Susan E., Thomas Brock, Adnan Moussa, and Xiaotao Ran. 2020. *Exploring the State of the Humanities in Community Colleges.* https://chatqa .com/media/k2/attachments/exploring-state-humanities-community -colleges.pdf.

Blikstein, Paulo, Sylvia Libow Martinez, Heather Allen Pang, and Kevin Jarrett, eds. 2016. *Meaningful Making: Projects and Inspirations for Fab Labs & Makerspaces.* Mountain View, CA: Constructing Modern Knowledge Press.

Deeken, Lynn, Meggan Press, Angie Thorpe Pusnik, Laura Birkenhauer, Nate Floyd, Lindsay Miller, Andrew Revelle, et al. 2019. "Navigating Student

Success: Learning from the Higher Education Landscape." *Reference Services Review* 47 (3): 7–23.

"Design Thinking: History." n.d. IDEO. Accessed June 28, 2021. https://designthinking.ideo.com/history.

Kuh, George D. 2008. *High-Impact Educational Practices: What They Are, Who Has Access to Them, and Why They Matter.* Washington, DC: American Association of Colleges and Universities.

Papert, Seymour. 1972. "Teaching Children Thinking." *Programmed Learning and Educational Technology* 9 (5): 245–55.

CHAPTER NINE

Sustaining the Partnership

Imagine that a visually impaired or blind library user goes to a reference librarian with a question at the reference desk about a resource the person is trying to use. It may be a database that can only be accessed visually to be used, and common screen readers cannot help the student interpret the information that is displayed. Perhaps an English literature major is attempting to review historic newspapers such as those in the Early English Books Online collection (EEBO). This may seem like an insurmountable barrier. Librarians may be well poised to assist in the process of inquiry, locating information, and citing information, but who can assist in making the resource accessible? While the publishers of such a resource are ultimately responsible, no student should be placed in this situation.

While the publisher or database provider works to meet the legal requirements to provide equitable access to the information, it may also be possible to collaborate with other on-campus units to provide a unique service to help facilitate the needs of such a student. The librarian can work with the campus accessibility team to help create a new service to meet the needs of visually impaired or blind students who need specific resources.

From the onset of any collaboration discussions to establishing a sustained partnership, taking care of the relationship is essential for shared success. In any successful collaboration, the units working together will meet the needs of the students within the scope and parameters of what is possible. And what is possible depends on the limitations of each unit, including time and other resources, but also meeting the unique goals of the units.

Fitting in projects and collaborations in order to grow the idea must help meet or achieve a goal in a college's or university's strategic plan. Each strategic plan will include goals, and there are usually additional goals at unit and college levels. In an ideal situation, all of the goals or needs for individual units will fulfill the overall strategic plan of the university and serve the students. Cross-unit teams are essential to looking at enrollment, retention, and student success.

In all collaborations, the administrators, directors, staff, and decision-makers of the individual units must be consulted and informed. As collaborative work to design new services can require resources, all administrators and budget owners must be able to contribute support. For projects or plans to come together, it's important to understand who is able to make decisions and which level of decision-making can be done at which level. This should be known prior to entering into a collaboration, but if individuals are unsure, it's important to engage and communicate with individuals in those units to make sure the plans meet the shared goals and that the appropriate decision-making has been enacted. This can look like individuals from each unit meeting with supervisors or colleagues who may be impacted by the change or the decisions.

Effective collaborations are accomplished in conducting research and environmental scans of the available information on the topic prior to deciding on a solution. Though this will begin through collecting anecdotes and stories from students, it will also include collecting data on the topic. Being open and listening intently to students and the barriers they face is the first step. Many ignore or avoid these kinds of conversations, thinking that there are many worldly conundrums that libraries and higher education cannot solve, but this is not the best way forward for all of us collectively. There are ways to make improvements through real analysis and deep listening. Collecting lists of barriers, either as mental lists or in documents, is one start to understanding what to do next. Identifying students' passions is another list to collect.

Determining Shared Needs

In working to look at the overlapping shared needs, it's important to consider if there are others who can become involved to assist in the project or plan, and how short or long term their commitments may be. Determining if the library can hire interns or students to help meet those needs is one avenue. Another method becoming more popular is to teach courses to solve community needs; students work in the class to identify and meet information needs.

As mentioned in chapter 7, community-based participatory approaches are a model for making positive changes and impact in the community being served. This work reflects an understanding of the health disciplines' approach to making improvements in health outcomes by involving the community. In Giachello et al.'s *Making Community Partnerships Work: A Toolkit* (2007), they suggest strategies to support the ongoing care of a partnership. They know that the care of the partnership—and the lengths to which that care goes—results in direct impact on the community. In other words, communities become healthy from healthy partnerships.

The tool kit makes several recommendations that form a preassessment to determine if partners are ready and prepared to serve a community. This includes evaluating whether the missions and visions of the partnerships are aligned: "Do your mission, culture, and priorities encourage, support and recognize the value of partnerships?" if the answer is no, that may not be a complete showstopper, but it must be addressed in terms of how one would work within such an environment.

Make sure that the intentions and the impact that the units can make is positive by asking a few key questions. First, looking at the landscape, are all of the partners present? If not, determine who is missing and see about inviting them to the conversations. Individual representatives from each area should be able to determine the goals and key performance indicators of each unit. For example, if one unit has the goal to get a certain percentage of students comfortable or able to use emerging technology, and another has a goal to graduate a certain percentage of students, the shared needs in terms of student success would be aligned. Both units would want to see the students engaged with the campus, involved in high-impact educational practices, and connecting with their community. These needs will differ across units and partners. To go back to the original example used in this chapter, if the unit responsible for students with disabilities has the goal to provide supports for disabled students to access and graduate from the university, and the library has the goal to support students' information access, designing a service that meets both needs is feasible, within this context.

Community-Based Participatory Research

Librarianship has recently explored the topic of participatory librarianship. Participatory librarianship is where the users of the library services work alongside the librarians to design, improve, and even implement the services offered. Community-based participatory research is very similar. As a form of action research, it's where the users of a service work side by side along with the partners to solve the problem at hand. According to Giachello et al. (2007), this is defined in the health partnership disciplines as "the method of involving community members in the research process. In CBPR, researchers and community members work side by side to identify a problem." Determining the levels to which one will include the community or library users in the delivery and design of the project is up to the partners and how roles are defined.

Defining the roles and setting up tasks and outcomes is covered in chapter 10. For this section, it's important to remember to start defining the type of partnership and exploring what services could possibly be delivered.

Networks are informal groups of individuals working toward a common cause. Networks may require the least amount of care to maintain due to the fact that they are not reliant on interdependence to deliver ongoing services. Coalitions, task forces, committees, and working groups are all on par with a similar set of ongoing responsibilities toward one another. This requires some additional commitment in order to maintain the group. Working groups sometimes form out of established networks. There are very formal types of partnerships which require memorandums of understanding as they involve resource commitments. Focusing on the grassroots collaborations, networks, working groups, and committees are the most viable long-term kinds of partnerships in higher education. They require minimal resources to start, and as a result, only require support for the partnership.

Ongoing Care of the Partnership

Once the partnership has been formed, and the members of the group have decided they want to move forward to explore options, they should discuss their shared vision. This may be as simple as easing the experience for students in certain situations or facing certain barriers. The vision may be to remove the barrier altogether, but this is the kind of goal that typically takes time. As such, it may make a great vision, a worthy cause that should be pursued, though the steps one would take to go about that vision could be insurmountable. If ending housing insecurity for students were the vision, one would take many steps to achieve this. In that circumstance, it would be necessary to discuss which steps would bring the partnership close to the goal.

As these conversations take place, involving students could be important through focus groups, design-thinking workshops, or meetings. In all of those cases, students should be compensated in whatever way possible. Incentives are not often included as a part of budgets, but in this case, partners can make an initial budget request to compensate students for their participation. It could also be useful to involve the voice of students through surveys or by hiring them to assist in the design of the project.

A recent trend in libraries is to hire students to work on a temporary project of evaluating projects or services. They may work only for a semester or for the summer to evaluate and improve a given project. Working on a project and paying students to work as a part of the project has a strong appeal. Hiring students as partners brings them directly into the work, provides them with agency over the services they use, and engages librarians in a participatory process. Research partnerships provide students with skills they can add to their resume. In essence, this supports their future success, too, while improving the services being delivered to students.

To encourage individuals to continually participate, there are several communication and performance strategies to employ. These include setting specific goals and tasks and making clear outcomes for the group to pursue. Keeping in communication with all of the individuals on an ongoing basis is crucial and should involve how they make decisions, what their expectations are, and how to build trust among group members.

Reference

Giachello, A. L., D. Ashton, P. Kyler, E. S. Rodriguez, R. Shanker, and A. Umemoto. 2007. *Making Community Partnerships Work: A Toolkit.* White Plains, NY: March of Dimes Foundation.

CHAPTER TEN

Collaboration between Units: Making Partnerships Work

When collaborating between units and groups, maintaining a regular flow of communication is critical. If there has been, historically, no previous relationship or no prior collaborations between the units, establishing a relationship organically with positive communication is essential to setting the stage. Students benefit when the collaborations work smoothly and there are no concerns within the units about these services. Due to this need, there are skills, methods, and processes that collaborators will want to learn and practice. Throughout this chapter, methods and techniques are presented that can enhance a library collaborator's understanding of the importance of ongoing collaborative communication.

These skills are foundational leadership and management abilities, as well as performance improvement metrics, that will benefit the individuals as well as the institutions in which they work. Acquiring and improving these skills to improve work for all individuals are a part of these collaborations. What follows throughout this chapter are methods and ideas to become acquainted on how to work together in ways that are equitable and fair. This work shares information about how to lead meetings, especially with an eye toward justice and power dynamics. Who has the final say on decisions as groups proceed to work together? How does the newly formed group come to a decision? What is the decision-making process? The group meeting can decide together how this will take place and revise or review the decision-making on a regular basis.

In all cases, it's important to understand that the way the individuals will work together must be stated from the outset. Collaborations can be most effective when working with specific criteria with respect to boundaries, scope, and desired outcomes. Feedback must be discussed early in the process, during the first several meetings, in order to achieve the desired outcome of working together well.

Establishing Meeting and Partnership Guidelines

It's important to set up agreements for how the groups will organize, lead, and deliver in order to achieve mutual success and deliver services to the students. While it will be normal for these agreements to change over time, this process of evaluation must be overt and consensus-driven, especially if the first agreements were made with a consensus model. A grassroots collaboration is such that the power dynamics are organically created. These groups can proceed with administrative support, but if they originate in a grassroots manner, the dynamics of power need to be clear.

The first item to discuss is when meetings will occur. The method of selecting times or choosing a routine time should become a part of the meeting guidelines for the group. These guidelines should include deciding how decisions will be made and what the roles of each group member will be. There are many examples of meeting guidelines, and the set we suggest comes from the nonprofit world. The Google document titled "Suggested Documents for Meeting Guidelines" ("Suggested Guidelines for Group Meetings" n.d.) comes from the nonprofit Resources for Social Change. In addition to setting the expectations and guidelines for meetings that take place for the partnership, the roles that need to be defined include who will set agendas, who facilitates or leads the meeting, and who prepares and organizes meeting materials. The more detail can be decided in advance, the better the meetings will flow, and disagreements will be able to be addressed.

Defining How to Set Meeting Expectations

The individuals meeting should first define how the group expectations will operate. They can set the standards for meeting guidelines. There are several examples of setting these kinds of guidelines; just as an example, they can include that the group wants to start the meeting and end on time at an established time or not have hidden agreements as they leave the meeting. Each individual should have a say with those cocreating the meeting agreements, and they should be decided by consensus. If a meeting guideline is not being followed, it's a good idea to set up in advance a method by which the group will address this. Keeping to the guidelines is important, as it establishes trust and keeps a solid and positive partnership. If this falls apart, it can impact the students.

The AORTA Anti-Oppressive Facilitation Guide (AORTA 2014) from the worker-owned co-op AORTA provides a great framework for addressing equity in meetings to ensure that all individuals can have a voice as the meetings take place. This is crucial in a situation where a partnership is being maintained, as individuals are all present voluntarily. In other words, partnerships are typically organized because the individuals want the outcome, but the partnership itself may not be a requirement of a job.

Some of the examples highlighted in this guide include shared agreements about how to show respect for one another. The meeting agreements and guidelines should be cocreated by all involved, and all should agree to follow them. Some suggested examples include, "no hidden disagreements" or "voice all concerns in the meeting" or "it's OK to slow the process down to address concerns."

Revise the guidelines as a group regularly. These meeting expectations will change. Depending on the length of the time of the project, or the collaboration, the group will want to decide how often to review and revise the meeting expectations. There are two important times to revise and reflect on meeting expectations. The first is a part of a regular review cycle. Annually may be an acceptable time frame. Weekly may not be an acceptable time frame, as it could get in the way of the work and the desired outcomes. Reviewing the guidelines weekly may also be acceptable if the work is deeply intensive, takes a lot of weekly time, and has a short time frame.

Deciding on a Facilitator

Roles are important in these meetings. Fulfilling those expectations as stated builds trust and continues the relationship. There may be a single facilitator, the facilitator can rotate among members of the group, or there can be roles divided among the members of the group. Depending on the culture of the organization or the groups you are working with, it may take more time than expected to have this conversation. It's best to discuss it upfront rather than down the line so that the collaborators have a basis for ongoing discussion that they can revisit when they want changes to be made.

A facilitator ensures that the group is working to meet the outcomes set forth and by the guidelines decided upon. All individuals working together have a shared obligation to conduct themselves and hold each other accountable to the agreed guidelines. The facilitator can set up meetings and monitor from a metaperspective the working health of the collaborations.

The facilitator is one of the key roles to decide first, as it will take on the responsibility of ensuring the group meets decided-upon outcomes. Without this, there may be a diffuse sense of responsibility, which can also lead to a natural dissipation of collaborating. It's up to the group to decide the level of formality necessary to achieve their desired goals. Some groups may form temporarily, others more long term. Again, it comes back to what the members want to achieve together.

Keeping in mind that the first few times you meet, you'll be discussing ideas, there may not be a need for a facilitator at that step. Once you've thought of an idea, and everyone involved decides that this is an action they would all like to take, then a facilitator will need to be appointed to make sure that folks involved are accountable to one another.

It's equally important to manage up and down in your organization, communicating with those who supervise your work, and those you supervise, in addition to the sideways conversations across units. Stakeholders above and below the collaborators always have questions about what it means for them in terms of the resources they have at their disposal. When the group has settled on a project, and once the project starts to have tasks associated with it, it may be time to decide on the project steps and roles.

Setting Roles

Problems in projects can originate with issues of communication. As a result, a strong focus on communication is key to setting the stage for successful collaborations. In the area of roles and who needs to be informed, that can be particularly tricky. Everyone wants to be the first to know information, and no one ever wants to be the last. With this in mind, when collaborating, it's important to outline who all the key stakeholders will be in those projects.

There are lots of mechanisms one can use to maintain effective methods of communication, and indeed, the entire field of communication explores this topic. In this section we present and suggest some methods you can use for collaborating, especially when it is the first time for two groups who have no previous history together. Grassroots collaboration is interesting for many reasons. For one, when groups are decided in a top-down model, often the communication is provided back to the administrators who directed employees to conduct the work. When employees on the ground providing services decide to collaborate, this creates new, trailblazing patterns of communication.

In an organization that is hierarchical in nature, if groups collaborate outside of the norm, it can create new dynamics of both power and communication. Who makes the decisions, and how? Who is responsible for carrying out the tasks? What can happen is the structures of the organization can be somewhat shifted. By holding intentional conversations around this, more individuals will feel engaged and satisfied with the outcomes, because the nature of the process itself was transparently discussed and perhaps moved toward a consensus-building model.

Regardless which decision-making process you adopt as collaborators, establishing roles is important. Allowing folks to self-select based on their interests, passions, and existing skills is necessary. While some individuals may have skills to offer, they may want to go in the direction of acquiring new skills. This can be supported. Though a person is known for skills in one area, it does not mean that that's what the person will want to do in the new collaboration.

To create a shared understanding of how the work will be divided and accomplished, it's important to establish some type of responsibility matrix. There are many variations of a responsibility matrix, and we will present the basic elements here. A responsibility matrix is a useful tool emerging from the field of project management. These are used to try to organize all of the collaborators, their roles, and responsibilities. Also called a responsibility assignment matrix, the simplest form of this is a list of individuals in a table, with the tasks across the top of the table and a letter or code representing their role in that step. A common way to create a responsibility matrix is to use one called a RACI Matrix or a Gantt Chart. In this case, RACI stands for "responsible, accountable, consulted, and informed." The responsible party must carry out the task, and there may be several folks who are responsible for the task. The person accountable makes sure the task has been completed. Folks may not be responsible or accountable for a task, but we may consult with them by checking in to solicit their opinions about decisions involved within that task. Finally, folks who are informed need to be kept in the loop.

When groups are collaborating and roles are not clear or defined, everyone will wonder about their own roles in the group, who is doing which aspect, and how they can help. Groups with ill-defined membership need this foundation in order that they may be successful. Again, this is all a matter to be decided. How the partners make decisions is important. Some adopt *Robert's Rules of Order* as a guideline—which is quite formal—and have a voting process. There are alternative Robert's Rules of Order that can be used as well (Susskind 1999), however, the authors recommend that those creating informal, grassroots partnerships and who conduct participatory and action research and use consensus decision-making.

Consensus Process and Organizational Support

Consensus decision-making is one of the most ethical and equitable methods for making decisions. When creating something new, getting the support from your peers and colleagues can be critical to the success of the project. Buy-in can be a by-product of consensus-driven decision-making. This is why creating a consensus-driven collaboration can be helpful. When bringing up new ideas, projects, services, or collaborations, sharing the ideas and asking for feedback early on will help create a better project overall, and the collaborators will benefit from the skills and expertise of others.

Though it is time-consuming, making decisions by consensus will ensure all concerns are addressed. Not everyone will want to use this process, as it can be slow, but it does take in all parties and their thoughts. This can lead to the best possible outcome in a partnership. There are some models that work to check to see if consensus is being followed and how to learn how to establish and get to consensus. Reaching consensus is different from consensus building in that it requires that all agree prior to moving forward. Consensus building is the act of checking with multiple stakeholders for perspectives and opinions, but it often results in forward movement without true consensus.

Many nonprofits utilize consensus, as it is a key tool for nonviolent decision-making where no action is taken unless all individuals agree. Food Not Bombs is a mutual aid group that offers a flowchart to use for consensus decision-making. In the Food Not Bombs model ("Food Not Bombs Consensus Process" n.d.), there are two passes for decision-making. In that process, individuals can either step aside or block a decision to go forward. Stepping aside refers to an individual disagreeing but not so substantially as to want to prevent the work from moving forward. Blocking is an action any individual can take. In a block, an individual can prevent the project from going forward. Individuals may do so for a number of reasons, but generally it is due to serious concerns regarding core values that were not adequately taken into perspective. This model gives each individual an equal part in the process. Since there is no majority rule or voting process, each individual's voice is powerful.

Shared Goals

Though discussing goals is something that ought to happen early on and throughout this process, establishing and understanding what each collaborating unit is trying to accomplish is important. Take the time to learn about the strategic plans in other units, and discuss what's most important to them. Having these conversations may unlock some key element of the process that has been missed. The best time to hold these kinds of conversations is when an event or action was disappointing and there is something a collaborator wishes could have happened but did not. These kinds of frustrations reveal a passion or desire to get to a larger goal. Through discussion, you can learn what might be the most beneficial way to solve the problems.

When you talk about your shared goals and strategic plans regularly, you keep the efforts and work top of mind. When you find common goals together through conversation, discovering shared goals can lead to the improved conversations. These conversations create insights about how to better reach those goals. Unlocking these ideas will better serve your students. This engagement leads to better retention of both the teams working to solve the issue and the students being served. No matter what, if you are working to better meet these goals, you are improving the services by learning more ways to improve and understand the issues at hand.

Celebrate Successes

Though we often overlook small successes, it is important to stop and celebrate accomplishing even the smallest of steps. Making progress toward an outcome, completing a step, or seeing your work benefit a student are all great examples of moments to celebrate.

When you see a moment you can celebrate, it's important to tell that story and showcase the work of others. Sharing out these stories will also help create additional collegial buy-in and support. By sharing the successes, folks will see this as working. This is true for both anecdotal stories and data. Data are something that can help individuals understand the significance of the impact of a new service model, but anecdotal stories of success can go much further.

When sharing out a success, especially when it is a student project or success, always check in with the folks whom you are celebrating to ask how they would want to be represented in such a context. Let them know if you'll be sharing the success by email team-wide or library-wide, or if you are asking for their consent to have their success be on your library website. Let them know, invite them into the process, and ask for their consent and permission to share the story. Individuals may have intellectual property rights over some of the content they are working on, may want to remain private, or they may have other reasons not to share. It's important to respect their choice and decision regardless of what that is.

Give shout-outs or microempowerments as celebrations to teammates who did something great. When talking about the work, sharing out stories of what someone did really well can be beneficial to everyone involved. Finally, it's important to follow these same consensus-driven steps when presenting work to ensure that everyone's voice is heard and they are representing the work in the ways they prefer.

References

"AORTA Anti-Oppressive Facilitation." 2014. AORTA. http://schadavis.org/wp-content/uploads/2015/02/ao_facilitation_resource_sheet_july_2014.pdf.

"Food Not Bombs Consensus Process." n.d. Food Not Bombs. Accessed June 30, 2021. http://foodnotbombs.net/new_site/PDF/CONSENSUS%20FLOW%20CHART.pdf.

"Suggested Guidelines for Group Meetings." n.d. Resources for Social Change. Accessed June 30, 2021. https://docs.google.com/document/d/16kC6dPV8rte3b8tNX6f-s7Y1IhkYBGkv5wNUnHZFmXQ/edit.

Susskind, Lawrence. 1999. "An Alternative to *Robert's Rules of Order* for Groups, Organizations, and Ad Hoc Assemblies That Want to Operate by Consensus." In *The Consensus Building Handbook*, edited by Lawrence Susskind, Sarah McKearnan, and Jennifer Thomas-Larmer, 3–57. Thousand Oaks, CA: SAGE.

PART 4

Conclusion

CHAPTER ELEVEN

Addressing Student Success Going Forward

A university and a library must always keep student success as the primary goal. As we work to identify ways to meet students' needs and provide support, we must also look at ways to broaden change systematically through policy and ongoing revision. Making a change to add new services is very important. It's equally important to create a healthy pattern of change and revision. There are continual changes and threats to student success. These must be addressed continuously.

Developing Partnerships and Services Model

In chapter 7, we articulate a process that takes in all of the knowledge presented in this book to go about designing more services for college students. It's important to realize that making change can happen simply by educating yourself about the users that your library serves. By deeply listening and paying attention to their needs, you can make connections with those students that will change their lives. The process can be followed in a cyclical fashion, testing ideas and learning more. It can also abruptly end, but the benefit is increased knowledge. Some partnerships may not succeed, but in the process, all involved will have learned a lot more about the students and the campus to become better educators.

Referring back to chapters 3 and 8 where emerging technologies are discussed, failure is a part of the process, and that's what research looks like. When partnerships or services do not work, they become the fertile soil for the future successes to grow.

Librarians ought to pay attention to student needs. This is best accomplished through a combination of anecdotes, stories from students, and data.

In that process, librarians can learn more about their true needs and whether or not the library can be in a position to meet those needs. Needing food or a home may not be something the library can provide directly. Access to partners who do provide those is an information need. In many cases, societal issues can be connected to information needs about what is available and from whom. A well-informed librarian is in the best position to assist in deciding how to meet the needs. If there are information needs or complex information problems to solve through opportunities, the library can be a very effective partner. By offering high-impact educational practices through services like makerspaces, the library can help pivot to support students' success. But, what about beyond the individual?

The Institution and Policy

Making these individual changes is important. It may not always be possible to take on positions of leadership and make systemic changes to pivot an entire library to focus on student success. In those cases, it is important to advocate and partner with institutions and individuals who write and draft policy.

Policy is how decisions are made at college, universities, libraries, and systems of higher education. As discussed earlier, another driver of change is that colleges face increased constraints from budgets and political movements. There are many pressures regarding priorities and resources for all units on college campuses. As a result, engaging in a regular process of revision and review as well as ensuring student engagement and success are critical. The health of an academic library and the educational institution it serves requires that they be as relevant as possible. The process of looking into information needs and creating new services to meet student needs is not a singular, one-time exercise. This process, if one engages in it authentically, will serve the institution with prepared data and review information for other existing, external demands. There are ways to go beyond this as well, by collaborating with external agencies and addressing systematic policy change at state and federal levels.

One example of such a policy change was discussed in chapter 6, the creation of the Washington Student Achievement Council. This agency was created through legislation and has led to policy changes at the state level. The Council has created significant directional progress to increase the number of evidence-based student success initiatives in Washington State. Through collaborations between institutions of higher education (as well as K–12), WSAC has advocated for, supported, and generated changes in policies affecting students. This kind of change can become more widespread and be re-created in other states. Campus collaborators can unite to fight for more policy change. Let's look into how they started.

The Washington Student Achievement Council (WSAC) was formed in 2012 with the express purpose of addressing equity gaps in higher education. The Washington State Legislature passed a bill modifying the previous Higher Education Coordinating Council and establishing the Washington Student Achievement Council with the express purpose of gaining strides in equitable access to higher education. According to the Washington State governor's website (Washington Governor Jay Inslee n.d.), the WSAC has this purpose: "Proposes goals for increasing educational attainment, the resources to support those goals, and the improvements and innovations to help meet the goals. The Council also advocates for increased commitment and resources for higher education and to link secondary and postsecondary education and training including the transition to careers." Since 2012, its members have worked to create policy changes at a systemic level applied throughout the state to help students meet their goals.

A significant policy goal is to conduct outreach and establish support to help students transition into higher education institutions. GEAR UP is a program designed to support high school students in gaining access to their desired colleges. In a policy recommendations document (Liang and Merkel 2013), WSAC policy analysts pinpoint some key areas to develop. Culture is one place where they want to make improvements: "To improve student achievement, Washington must develop a culture that expects and assists the pursuit of postsecondary credentials and helps students through critical academic transition points." The policy recommendations include substantial outreach to at-promise students.

The WSAC recommends a set of actions to go about achieving this work. Providing for a systematic distribution of educational materials can help all students be on the same playing field about the processes involved in applying to college. Finding mentors for students is critically important as well, to help get the students through some of the difficult aspects of the process and also to celebrate successes. Another recommendation is to make personal connections to provide methods of support during transition, a moment when students may feel most marginalized and need some celebrations.

Librarians can be a part of this discussion and assist in the information dissemination aspects. In addition, librarians can work as mentors and make personal connections with the students to support them through their journey. Librarians can also take action with other staff and faculty to advocate to establish policy such as this in their own states or institutions.

An example of where librarians can make significant change is with the adoption of Open Educational Resources, or OER, which are low-cost and affordable learning materials for courses. There are many agencies and state boards of education that have adopted frameworks for lowering the cost of textbooks for courses in higher education.

In the case of WSAC, the council discusses all of the possibilities for outcomes through policy suggestions. In conversation at meetings, they review the possible policies and make decisions about which ones they can support, or find resources to support, and which would have prioritized outcomes.

They decide which metrics to establish in order to meet those goals. Certainly, having this kind of a statewide policy group is a substantial move; nonetheless, creating a similar group at a local or institutional level is possible. Faculty and staff senates at colleges and universities are one place to go about initiating conversations about how to advance student success at systems thinking levels.

Starting the Discussion at Your Library

> There comes a point where we need to stop just pulling people out of the river. We need to go upstream and find out why they're falling in.
> —Desmond Tutu

It is favorable to assume that all individuals working in an academic library would be doing so to benefit students and to promote student success. Each individual may have a combination of intrinsic and extrinsic motivations. Some brief recommendations can help support starting this conversation at your library.

If you become passionate about the topic, make it your own personal research interest. You can publish on it, learn more, and present your work to colleagues. Another avenue is to find a group of like-minded individuals within the library to work on external partnerships. This can always begin as a reading group or as a professional development meeting designed to work together. Having conversations within the library can lead to more work on this topic over time.

Using this book and understanding the background of at-promise students is a beginning. At different times, individuals all feel either marginalized or as if they belong. This is true of colleagues as much as it is about students. As a final call to action, developing empathy and understanding for all students, creating services and making connections that benefit them, and advocating for their well-being are all key to developing students who are successful and able to complete their academic pursuits.

References

Liang, Weiya, and Vicki Merkel. 2013, October 8. "September Meeting Minutes." Washington Student Achievement Council. https://wsac.wa.gov/sites /default/files/2013.10.08.00.September.Meeting.Minutes.pdf.
Washington Governor Jay Inslee. n.d. "Student Achievement Council, Washington." Accessed July 1, 2022. https://www.governor.wa.gov/boards-commissions /board-and-commissions/profile/Student%20Achievement%20Council %2C%20Washington.

Index

About the Authors

Amy E. Vecchione is a professor and assistant director of research and innovation at eCampus Center, Boise State University. She has authored articles on emerging technologies and student success for the past 15 years. Vecchione is the winner of the President's Community Service Award in 2020 from Boise State University for her work finding creative, engaging, community-based solutions during the pandemic.

Cathlene E. McGraw is an academic advisor at the New Jersey Institute of Technology. She earned a BA in journalism from the University of Oregon and an MS in college student services from Oregon State with a focus on working with at-risk/at-promise students. McGraw served students and faculty as the director of queer student services at Portland State, where she found her passion for academic advising.